Oriental Papercrafts

Oriental
Papercrafts

25 beautiful Eastern-inspired projects

Cheryl Owen

NEW
HOLLAND

First published in 2008 by New Holland Publishers (UK) Ltd
London • Cape Town • Sydney • Auckland

Garfield House
86–88 Edgware Road
London W2 2EA
United Kingdom
www.newhollandpublishers.com

80 McKenzie Street
Cape Town 8001
South Africa

Unit 1, 66 Gibbes Street
Chatswood
NSW 2067
Australia

218 Lake Road
Northcote
Auckland
New Zealand

ISBN 978 1 84773 075 6

Senior Editor: Emma Pattison
Designer: Zoe Mellors
Photographer: Paul Bricknell
Production: Hazel Kirkman
Editorial Direction: Rosemary Wilkinson

1 3 5 7 9 10 8 6 4 2

Repro by Pica Digital PTE Ltd, Singapore
Printed and bound by Times Offset (M) Sdn Bhd, Malaysia

contents

Introduction

Oriental designs lend themselves beautifully to papercrafts, although this is hardly surprising as paper was invented by the Chinese. Exquisite papers are still produced in China and Japan using ancient techniques and paper has featured in many oriental festivals, from illuminated lanterns to kite flying, for centuries.

Origami, the Japanese art of paper folding, usually springs to mind when thinking of oriental papercrafts but there are lots of other fascinating techniques. This book presents traditional projects that still look fresh and new as well as contemporary applications using lovely papers. Many classic oriental papercrafts have spiritual connections which will add an extra element if you are making a project to give as a gift. There is such a huge range of stunning papers available today that the possibilities of creating with this wonderful material are endless.

Materials, equipment and techniques

This section presents the wonderful choice of materials available for oriental papercrafts and outlines the basic equipment required. All of the techniques used for the projects are easy-to-follow and quick to master.

Materials

This section includes everything you

will need to create the stunning

papercrafts in this book.

Paper

Specialised and handmade Japanese papers are now widely available and although some are expensive, a single sheet can be used for many projects. Of course, you do not have to use authentic oriental papers – there is such a lovely variety of paper available today that you can use whatever takes your fancy as long as it is suitable for its application. The Japanese word for paper is 'washi'.

ABOVE *Craft papers printed with Chinese and Japanese designs give an instant feel of the orient.*

BELOW *Translucent Japanese papers often have interesting textures.*

PATTERNED PAPERS
Fantastic patterned papers featuring traditional Japanese designs are still created using techniques that have been used for centuries. These exquisite papers are often expensive because of the skills needed to produce them. Chiyogami, for example, is a decorative paper printed with wooden blocks. Many have small patterns, making them suitable for origami techniques.

MULBERRY OR KOZO PAPER
This versatile paper is surprisingly strong. There are short fibres distributed throughout the paper. Mulberry paper is inexpensive and widely available in a range of colours.

JAPANESE HIKAKUSHI
This delicately textured paper comes in a small range of subtle colours. It can be applied to card to strengthen it and then used as a background for greeting cards.

ECHIZEN WASHI
This very elegant paper is scattered with silky fibres and often incorporates metallic fragments.

JAPANESE ASARAKUSHI
This random mesh-like paper looks great applied over a contrasting colour. For best results apply this paper with spray adhesive as any other adhesive will be visible

MIZUTAMASHI PAPER

The pattern of holes is created by shooting fine jets of water at the paper while it is being made. Apply Mizutamashi paper with spray adhesive.

CRAFT PAPERS

Books are available featuring printed papers of various themes such as kimono fabrics that can be cut-up for craftwork. Craft shops sell A4 size (US Letter) and 30.5 cm (12 in) square sheets of printed papers and vellums.

ORIGAMI PAPER

These square sheets of patterned and plain papers are sold in packs for origami projects. They are very appealing as no other materials or equipment are required for traditional origami techniques. Origami papers are 15 cm (6 in) or 10 cm (4 in) square.

TISSUE PAPER

Use this inexpensive, lightweight paper to make imitation flowers. Layers of tissue paper can be joined to create a honeycomb effect (see the Chinese dragon on page 66)

RIGHT *Tissue and crepe papers are readily available at low costs.*

CREPE PAPER

This humble paper, reminiscent of school projects, is cheap to buy. It has a distinctive grain and can be stretched to curve the surface, such as in the lanterns on page 26.

RIGHT *Use expensive Japanese papers for special projects.*

Card

Card forms the basis of many paper creations, especially when making greeting cards. Coloured card is inexpensive and usually coloured throughout. Card with special coatings on one side such as pearlised or metallic finishes are very effective.

Stencil board

Use this oiled card to make stencils. The treated surface stops paint seeping through.

Mounting board

Construct boxes from mounting board. Always cut mounting board with a craft knife as using a pair of scissors will squash the surface.

ABOVE Coloured card forms the basis for many papercrafts.

Felt pens

Felt tip pens are available in lots of colours including metallics. They are a fast way of applying colour if you are nervous about using paint.

Paints

Acrylic paints are very versatile, the colours mix easily and dry quickly. Use watercolour paints on watercolour paper – the colours blend effortlessly together to create some great effects. Relief paints are fun to use. They come in a plastic tube and are applied through a thin nozzle.

LEFT Create colour with acrylic paints, felt pens, relief paints and watercolour paints.

Rubber stamps

Rubber stamps come in every imaginable theme and there are lots of oriental designs to choose from. Rubber stamps are easy to use and give a professional finish to a project. Stamp the designs with an ink pad.

RIGHT Stamp oriental images with rubber stamps and ink pads to create a design quickly.

Adhesives

Read the manufacturer's instructions for adhesives and test them on scrap paper before use. Spray adhesive gives an even coating of adhesive so is good for large areas. Always use spray adhesives in a well-ventilated room or outdoors and protect the surrounding area with old newspaper.

All-purpose household glue is useful for sticking small areas – use a cocktail stick to apply a tiny amount of glue. PVA (white) glue is a versatile, non-toxic glue. It can be thinned with water to make papier mâché. Glue dots are dots of glue on a backing tape or sheet. They come in various sizes and will stick small items quickly as no drying time is needed. Micro dots, as the name suggests, are little dots of glue. They come on a backing sheet and are used to stick tiny, intricate pieces.

Double-sided tape comes in various widths. It is a clean and neat way of joining layers of paper and card together. Use paper glue to stick paper and card together. Use flower tape to make paper flowers. It is available from florists in a limited range of colours, green and brown being the most versatile colours for flower making. Its waxy surface sticks to itself and is used to bind stems and wires. Use masking tape to stick templates and work temporarily in place. Use a low-tack tape and check beforehand that it will not tear or mark the work.

ABOVE *Always use the right adhesive for the task. There is a large range to choose from.*

Cords, threads and wire

Join paper and card with cords, threads and wire for practical purposes or purely for decoration.

MIZUHIKI

Mizuhiki is a twisted paper cord originally used as a fastening. It has many practical and decorative uses. Mizuhiki comes in lots of colours in lengths about 90 cm (36 in) long.

MEMORY CORD

This narrow cord is made of fine wire tightly bound with coloured thread. It maintains its shape once manipulated.

EMBROIDERY THREADS

If you are a keen needle-worker, you will already have lots of coloured embroidery threads. These can be used to bind books, make tassels and even embroider paper.

LINEN THREAD

Use linen thread to bind books and to sew coins and tokens as a finishing touch to projects.

WIRE

Wire is very useful for many craft applications as it can be manipulated into different shapes. For example, use thick wire to make stems for paper flowers. Fine coloured wires are fun to use for craftwork.

LEFT Gather together a selection of enticing embellishments for your papercraft projects.

Embellishments

It is the finishing touches that make a project extra special. Choose embellishments for their sparkle or distinctive touch of the orient.

BEADS

Just a single oriental bead such as a carved lacquer bead is a lovely finishing touch to a project. Ceramic beads with Chinese calligraphy painted on or beads made from real or imitation bone are a delightful feature. String beads with large holes on cord or embroidery threads.

SEQUINS

Sequins are inexpensive and add shine and sparkle to a project. Most sequins are round but other shapes such as flowers and shells are available and are very effective. Stick sequins with glue dots.

CHINESE COINS AND TOKENS

Imitation coins and tokens are available inexpensively at craft shops. Chinese coins are a symbol of prosperity, the square in their centre represents the energy of the earth.

CHOPSTICKS AND WOODEN SKEWERS

Although not usually associated with papercrafts, chopsticks immediately add an oriental look to a project. Use wooden skewers to manipulate models such as the Chinese dragon on page 66.

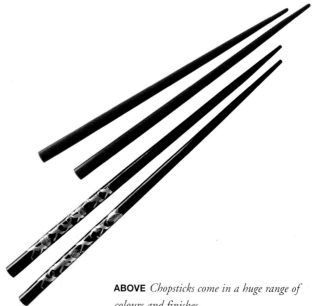

ABOVE Chopsticks come in a huge range of colours and finishes.

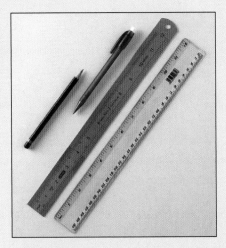

Equipment

Work on a clean, flat, well-lit surface for comfort

and safety. Always keep sharp tools and glues

beyond the reach of children and pets.

For drawing

An HB pencil is best for drawing. Keep pencils sharpened to a point or use a propelling pencil. Draw squares and rectangles with a ruler and set square so that the lines are straight and angles accurate. Describe circles with a compass or use a circle stencil for small circles.

For sticking

Spread glue with a plastic glue spreader or improvise and use a scrap of card. Use a cocktail stick to apply a tiny amount of glue accurately. A pair of tweezers are useful for applying small glued items. Alternatively, support them on the tip of a craft knife blade.

For applying paint

Paint with good quality artist's paintbrushes and clean the brushes immediately after use. Stencil with a flat ended stencil brush.

For sewing

Use a needle with a large eye to sew through paper and card and to thread cord. A length of fine wire folded in half with the ends twisted together can be used to pull cord and threads through beads.

LEFT *You may already have basic papercraft equipment.*

For cutting and scoring

Craft knives cut neatly and are better than scissors for cutting straight lines, especially on card. Cut with a craft knife on a cutting mat which has a self-healing surface. Change the knife blade frequently as a blunt blade will tear paper and card. Cut straight edges with a craft knife against a metal ruler. Retract the knife blade when it is not in use and always take care when handling the blades.

Choose scissors that are comfortable to handle and suitable for left- or right-handers appropriately. You may find it easier to cut intricate shapes such as small circles with a small pair of scissors rather than a craft knife.

Card can be scored with the back of a craft knife but for best results, use a bone folder. This traditional book binder's tool will dent the surface of the card but not cut and therefore weaken it. Crease along a fold with a bone folder to sharpen it.

Paper punches are available in lots of different designs and will punch out decorative shapes. Apply punched paper shapes with micro dots or paper glue.

It is often necessary to punch holes for fastening. Use a standard desk double hole punch to punch pairs of holes or a single hole punch for single holes. A hole puncher is available with different sized heads to punch different sized holes. Use a bradawl, resting on a cutting mat to pierce holes.

Snip wire with wire snippers or an old pair of scissors, bearing in mind that the metal will blunt scissor blades. Manipulate wire with a small pair of pliers – round-nose pliers are a versatile shape to use.

RIGHT *Always store and handle cutting equipment carefully.*

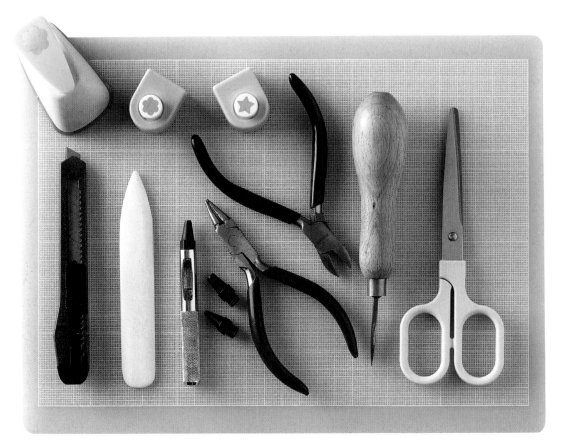

Techniques

This section describes the basic techniques that occur throughout the book. Always read the instructions for a project before embarking upon it and experiment with new techniques on scrap materials first. Follow metric or imperial measurements but not a combination of both.

Transferring templates

Trace the template onto tracing paper. Turn the tracing over and re-draw it on the wrong side with a pencil. Tape the tracing right-side -up on your chosen paper or card with masking tape. Re-draw the design to transfer it to the paper. Remove the tracing.

Scoring

Scoring the surface of card makes it easier to fold and gives a neat finish. A bone folder (see page 16) is recommended for scoring. Score with the pointed end against a ruler. The right or wrong side of the card can be scored. The bone folder will indent a line to fold along without breaking the surface. Alternatively, lightly score the card with the back of a craft knife, taking care to break the top surface only but not to cut right through the card.

Positioning motifs

To judge the placing of one or more motifs accurately, tape a tracing of the design to the background paper or card with masking tape. Apply adhesive to the back of the motif and slip it under the tracing, matching its position. Stick the motif in place. Carefully remove the tracing.

Strengthening paper

Applying paper to card with spray adhesive will strengthen the paper. Cut the paper approx- imately 1 cm ($^3/_8$ in) larger all round than the required size. Apply spray adhesive to the back of the paper then stick the paper on to the card, smoothing it outwards from the centre.

Using glue dots
Stick small items in place with glue dots. Press the item to the glue dot then lift it off the backing tape and press in position.

Using micro dots
Apply tiny and intricate items in place with micro dots. Press the item to the adhesive sheet. Peel off the item and press it in place.

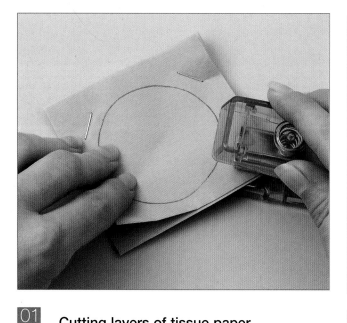

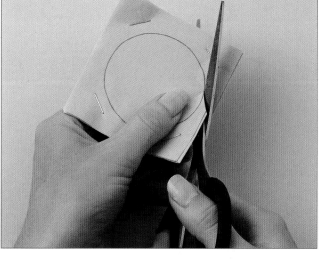

01 **Cutting layers of tissue paper**
Fold the layers in concertina pleats or cut pieces of tissue paper about 1.2 cm (1/2 in) larger all round than the motif. (Do not use more than twelve layers in one go.)

02 Draw the motif on the top layer with a pencil. Staple the layers together around the motif then cut out the motif with a pair of scissors.

01 **Making a tassel**
Cut a rectangle of card – 15 x 8 cm (6 x 3¼ in)
is a versatile size. Fold the card in half, parallel
with the short edges. Bind yarn around the card.

02 Fold a length of yarn in half and thread the ends
through the eye of a blunt needle. Slip the needle
behind the strands close to the fold then insert the
needle through the loop of the yarn and pull tightly.

03 Slip the tips of a pair of scissors between the
card layers and cut through the strands. Discard
the card.

04 Thread the needle with a single length of yarn
and bind it tightly around the head of the tassel,
securing the start of the yarn as you bind. To
secure, insert the needle into the bulk of the
tassel to lose the end of the yarn within the
tassel. Cut the tassel ends level.

The projects

This section presents twenty-five fantastic projects which

show how varied and versatile oriental papercrafts are.

From greeting cards and gift tags to lanterns and mobiles,

there's something here for everyone.

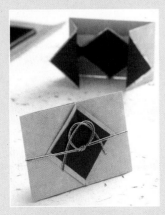

Kimono greeting card

Kimono literally means 'things to wear' and has been a traditional Japanese woman's garment since the eighth century. These beautiful robes with their distinctive long hanging sleeves are an inspiring shape to recreate for papercraft projects. This kimono-shaped greeting card is made with a gorgeous Japanese patterned paper and trimmed with sequins, embroidery thread and beads. The greeting card fits a standard size envelope.

YOU WILL NEED

Japanese patterned paper,
* 40 x 20 cm (15¾ x 8 in)*
Red card, 45 x 25 (18 x
* 10 in)*
Spray adhesive
Craft knife
Metal ruler
Cutting mat
Tracing paper
Masking tape
Pencil
Bone folder
Ruler
5 mm (¼ in) wide double
* sided tape*
2 flower shaped sequins
Bradawl
Large eyed needle
Stranded cotton embroidery
* thread*
Two 4 mm (⅙ in) red beads

01 Apply Japanese patterned paper to red card with spray adhesive. Cut the covered card to a 35 x 15.5 cm (13¾ x 6⅛ in) rectangle with a craft knife and metal ruler, resting on a cutting mat. Cut out the template on page 122 from tracing paper. Tape the template on one half of the covered card with masking tape and draw around it lightly with a pencil.

02 Score along the fold-line with a bone folder against a ruler, breaking the scoring at the collar. Resting on a cutting mat, cut around the collar with a craft knife, cutting the straight lines against a metal ruler.

03 Cut the front slits with a craft knife, cutting against a metal ruler. Fold the card in half along the scored line. Resting on a cutting mat, cut out the kimono with a craft knife, cutting against a metal ruler.

04 Cut a 9 x 1 cm (3$^1/_2$ x $^3/_8$ in) strip of red card for the collar bands. Trim the strip to fit the bands and stick to the kimono with 5 mm ($^1/_4$ in) wide double sided tape. Open the card out flat.

05 Stick a flower shaped sequin to the dots with tiny pieces of double sided tape. Resting on a cutting mat, pierce a hole in the card through the hole in the sequins with a bradawl.

VARIATION

This elegant greeting card in shades of purple uses a delicate metallic paper and is trimmed with shell shaped sequins and purple beads.

06

Thread the needle with six strands of stranded cotton embroidery thread. Insert the needle through one sequin and out through the other. Tie the embroidery thread in a knot between the sequins. Thread a red bead onto each end of the thread. Knot the thread under the bead. Cut off the excess thread.

Tasselled lantern

Make a set of colourful lanterns to decorate a party. Lanterns are used in all Chinese celebrations and the most wonderful examples can be seen at the Lantern Festival which is held in the first month of the Chinese New Year. For obvious reasons, the lanterns represent light and warmth. Crepe paper is cleverly pleated to create the popular lantern shape, and an elegant hanging tassel is suspended from the circular base. The lanterns fold flat so can be stored for future use, although they are so pretty that you may want to keep them up all year.

YOU WILL NEED

*Crepe paper, 30 x 20 cm
    (12 x 8 in)
Pencil
Ruler
Paper glue
Patterned giftwrap, 25 x
    15 cm (10 x 6 in)
White card, 25 x 15 cm
    (10 x 6 in)
Spray adhesive
Bradawl
Rayon embroidery thread
Needle
Scrap paper, 25 x 15 cm
    (10 x 6 in)
Paper glue
26 cm (10¹/₄ in) fine wire*

TIP

*Rayon embroidery thread is prone to curling.
Moisten the thread to straighten it.*

Cut a 25 x 18 cm (10 x 7¹/₂ in) rectangle of crepe paper, cutting the short edges parallel with the grain of the paper. On the wrong side, use a pencil and ruler to draw lines across the paper at 1.5 cm (⁵/₈ in) intervals parallel with the long edges. This will make the paper easier to fold.

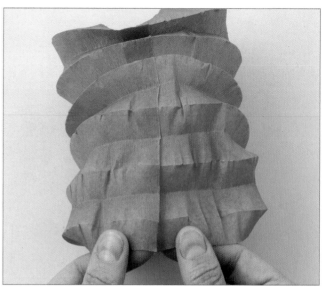

02 Fold the paper in concertina pleats along the drawn lines, starting by folding along the first line with wrong sides facing. With the right sides uppermost, pinch one of the upper folds together and gently stretch the fold between your fingers. Repeat on all the upper folds.

03 Open out the pleats at the short edges. Overlap the short edges by 1 cm ($^3/_8$ in) and stick together with paper glue, matching the folds of the pleats. Refold the pleats to flatten the lantern into a ring.

04 Apply patterned giftwrap to white card with spray adhesive. Refer to the template on page 122 to cut two circles from the covered card – cut out the inner circle on one piece. Pierce a hole at the dots. Refer to the Making a Tassel technique on page 19 to make a 9 cm ($3^1/_2$ in) long tassel from rayon embroidery thread. Knot the hanging threads together 12 cm ($4^3/_4$ in) above the tassel.

05 Thread the hanging threads onto a needle. Insert the needle through the hole in the centre of the card circle and make a double knot on the wrong side of the circle. Cut off the excess threads.

06 Resting on scrap paper, apply paper glue to the outer 1 cm (³/₈ in) of the tasselled circle on the wrong side. Stick the circle on top of the lantern with 2 mm (¹/₁₆ in) of the circumference of the lantern extending beyond the circumference of the tasselled circle.

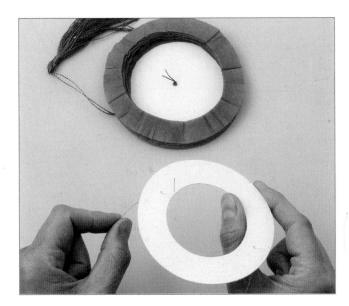

07 Bend 1 cm (³/₈ in) at each end of a 26 cm (10¹/₄ in) length of fine wire outwards at right angles. Resting on scrap paper, apply paper glue to the outer 1 cm (³/₈ in) of the remaining covered circle on the wrong side. Insert the bent ends of the wire through the pierced holes. Turn the lantern over and stick the covered circle at the other end of the lantern.

VARIATION

Coloured crepe paper can be decorated by painting it with household bleach to remove the colour. The deep blue crepe paper on this smart lantern has a pattern of diamond shapes painted with bleach. The card circles are covered with red mulberry paper and an oriental bead is threaded onto the hanging threads of a shiny tassel of gold embroidery thread.

Papier mâché bowl

Newspaper used for papier mâché is often painted over to disguise its humble origins but this simple bowl shows off the calligraphy of a Chinese newspaper to great effect. A rim of red mulberry paper makes a good contrast to the black and white newsprint.

YOU WILL NEED

Chinese newspaper,
   approximately 8 sheets
Plastic bowl to use as a
   mould, approximately
   17 cm (6¾ in) diameter
Petroleum jelly
PVA glue
Flat paintbrush
Black pen
Scissors
Red mulberry paper, 30 x
   25 cm (12 x 10 in)

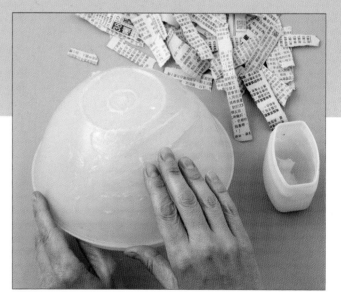

01 Tear black and white pages of a Chinese newspaper into strips about 2 cm (³/₄ in) wide. Smear the outside of an upturned bowl with petroleum jelly which will act as a releasing agent for the papier mâché.

02   Mix pva glue with a little water until it has the consistency of single cream. With a flat paintbrush brush the solution onto the strips and lay them smoothly on the bowl, overlapping the edges. Cover the bowl with the overlapped strips.

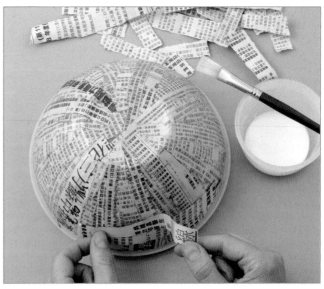

03   Continue building up layers of the papier mâché, laying each layer in a different direction to the last for strength. Leave to dry after you have applied twelve layers of papier mâché.

04   Draw a line with a black pen along the lower edge of the bowl – this will be the rim of the finished bowl. Carefully lift off the papier mâché bowl and wipe off the petroleum jelly. Cut away the excess papier mâché along the drawn line with a pair of scissors.

05   Tear red mulberry paper into strips about 2 cm (³/₄ in) wide and 3 cm (1¹/₄ in) long. Brush the PVA solution onto the rim of the bowl and lay the strips smoothly over the rim, overlapping the edges. Brush on more of the PVA solution after each strip is applied. Set aside to dry.

VARIATION

Chinese shops sell fake money which is fun to use for papier mâché. The fake money used for this shapely bowl is printed in red and blue on one side and green on the other and has has been applied in this way on the mould.

Stencilled butterfly kite

YOU WILL NEED

Stencil board, 40 x 30 cm
  (16 x 12 in)
Cutting mat
Craft knife
Metal ruler
Pale pink paper, 2 sheets,
  40 x 30 cm (16 x 12 in)
Deep pink paper, 20 x 10
  (8 x 4 in)
Deep pink, aquamarine, pale
  pink, yellow and light blue
  acrylic paint
Masking tape
Stencil brush
Kitchen towels
Pencil
Paper glue
Bradawl
3 wooden skewers
Aquamarine stranded cotton
  embroidery thread
Large eyed needle
1.5 cm (⁵/₈ in) diameter
  plastic curtain ring
30 cm (12 in) of turquoise
  craft wire
2 x 8 mm (⁵/₁₆ in) orange
  beads
2 x 2 cm (³/₄ in) gold sequins
Glue dots

Kites are flown at various oriental festivals as they have been for centuries. They usually depict motifs from the natural world and are made using traditional techniques. This pretty kite is not intended to be flown but would look superb displayed against a wall; there is a ring at the back to hang it up. The details are stencilled with bright paints and the butterfly is finished with a pair of sequin eyes and beaded wire antennae.

01 Use the template on page 123 to transfer the butterfly wing and body to stencil board (see page 17). Resting on a cutting mat, cut out the stencils with a craft knife, cutting the straight edge against a metal ruler. Tape the wing stencil to pale pink paper and the body stencil to deep pink paper with masking tape.

TIP

Clean and dry the stencil brush well before using a different colour paint.

35

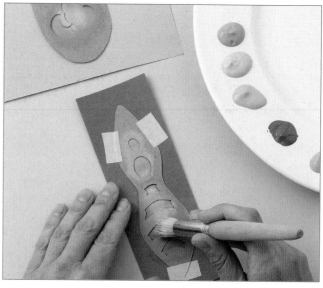

02 To stencil the wing, pick up a small amount of deep pink paint with a stencil brush. Dab off the excess paint on a kitchen towel. Dab the paint through the band cut-outs, holding the brush upright and moving it in a circular motion. Stencil the clouds on the wing and stripes on the body with aquamarine paint. Stencil the ovals on the body with pale pink paint. Leave to dry.

03 Stencil the centre of the bands on the wing and the centre of the ovals on the body with yellow paint. Stencil the oval on the wing, the centre and one edge of the clouds and the centre of the stripes on the body with light blue paint. Draw around the stencils with a pencil. Remove the stencils. Turn the wing stencil over and tape it to pale pink paper. Stencil the second wing. Draw around the wing.

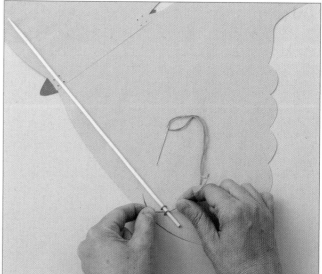

04 Cut out the wings and body. Run a line of paper glue along the straight edge of one wing on the right side. Overlap the straight edge of the wings by 1.5 cm ($^5/_8$ in) and stick together. Stick the body on top with paper glue. Resting on a cutting mat, pierce a hole at the dots with a bradawl. Turn the butterfly wrong side up.

05 Hold a wooden skewer between the dots on the body and one wing at the upper edge with the blunt end of the skewer pointing outwards. Sew the skewer to the wing through the pierced holes with a needle and embroidery thread, oversewing the skewer on the wrong side so that a cross stitch appears on the right side. Knot the thread ends together. Repeat on the other wing.

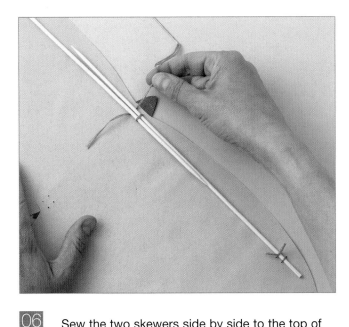

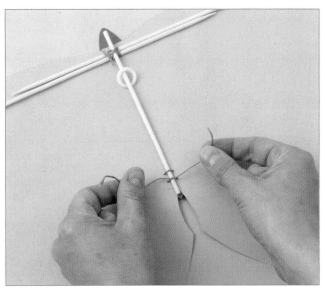

06 Sew the two skewers side by side to the top of the body through the pierced holes with a needle and embroidery thread, oversewing the skewers on the wrong side so that a cross stitch appears on the right side. Do not fasten the threads yet.

07 Trim a wooden skewer to 14 cm (5½ in) long. Hold the skewer between the dots on the body. Sew in place at the upper pierced holes with a cross stitch on the wrong side, fasten the threads securely. Slip a 1.5 cm (⅝ in) diameter plastic curtain ring onto the skewer and sew the other end through the lower pierced holes so that a cross stitch appears on the right side.

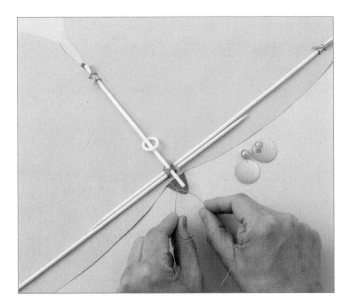

08 Slip the wire around the skewer intersection. Adjust the wire ends to extend evenly each side and twist them together twice above the body for antennae. Slip a bead onto each end and twist the wires together under the beads. Stick two 2 cm (¾ in) gold sequins to the top of the body as eyes with glue dots.

Origami boxes

This trio of colourful boxes is constructed with simple origami folding techniques and need no adhesive to hold the shape. The boxes will fit one inside the other. The box can be made in any size. The finished container will be a third of the size of the square of paper it is made from. For example, the largest box and lid shown here starts with 27 cm (10$\frac{1}{2}$ in) squares of paper which make a 9 cm (3$\frac{1}{2}$ in) square box. The middle size box and lid starts with 21 cm (8$\frac{1}{4}$ in) squares of paper which make a 7 cm (2$\frac{3}{4}$ in) square box and the small box and lid starts with 15 cm (6 in) squares of paper which make a 5 cm (2 in) square box.

YOU WILL NEED

Selection of six plain and patterned kozo papers, 27 cm (10½ in) square

01 Cut two squares of paper for the box and lid. Refer to the diagrams on page 123 to fold the squares along the solid and broken lines with the wrong sides facing. Open the squares out flat again. Refold the paper for the box diagonally in half. Fold the corners at the end of the diagonal fold inwards along the broken lines.

02 Stand the corners upright along the broken lines then fold them flat, matching the diagonal fold line to the broken lines. Crease along the new folds. Open the paper out flat and repeat on the other diagonal fold.

03 With the wrong side facing upwards, fold the box paper along two adjacent base lines to form two sides of the box. Bring the broken lines together, folding the excess paper at the corner inside.

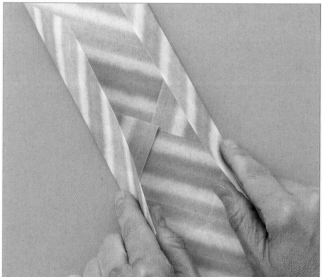

04 Fold the triangle at the top of the box corner over the corner to hold the corner in place. Re-crease along the corner fold to define it. Repeat to form the other corners of the box.

05 With the wrong side facing upwards, fold two opposite corners of the paper for the lid to meet at the centre. Fold again so that the broken lines meet at the centre.

VARIATION

Use squares of origami papers to make a box to present a gift of jewellery nestling in shredded tissue.

06 Lift the edges along the last pair of folds to form two opposite sides of the lid. Lift and fold the third side of the lid by bringing the third broken line level with the upright sides, folding the excess paper inwards at the corners.

07 Repeat with the fourth broken line on the fourth side. Fold down along the broken lines so that the points meet at the centre, on the underside of the lid.

Blue willow
paper cut

The blue willow is familiar as a popular pattern for tableware, making this charming cut-work picture a great choice to hang in a dining room. The picture fits a standard 22 x 16 cm ($8^3/_4$ x $6^1/_2$ in) picture frame. The design is inspired by the Chinese myth of star-crossed lovers, Koong-Lee and Chang, who met and fell in love beneath a willow tree. Upon their deaths, the gods turned them into a pair of immortal love birds.

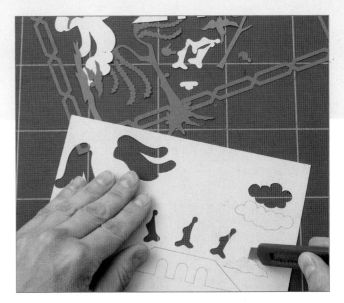

YOU WILL NEED

Cutting mat
Mid blue, light blue and
 white paper, 25 x 20 cm
 (10 x 8 in)
Craft knife
Metal ruler
Scrap paper
Paper glue
Tracing paper, 25 x 20 cm
 (10 x 8 in)
Masking tape
Spray adhesive
22 x 16 cm ($8^3/_4$ x $6^1/_2$ in)
 picture frame

01 Resting on a cutting mat, refer to the template on page 122 to cut the pieces from mid blue and light blue paper. Cut the light blue pieces along the broken lines with a craft knife and the straight lines against a metal ruler.

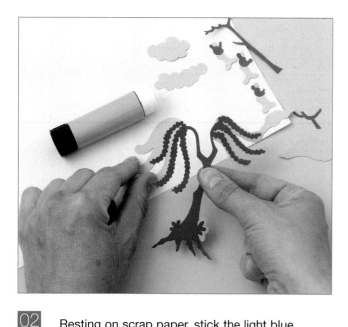

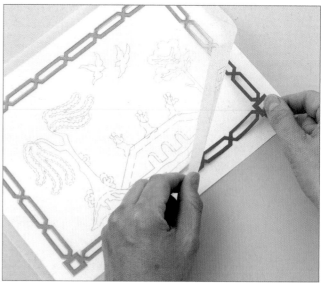

02 Resting on scrap paper, stick the light blue pieces behind the mid blue tree pieces and the mid blue pieces on the light blue people with paper glue.

03 Stick a tracing of the template to a 24 x 18 cm (9$\frac{1}{2}$ x 7$\frac{1}{4}$ in) rectangle of white paper with masking tape on the top edge. Spray the wrong side of the border with spray adhesive. Slip the border under the tracing and adjust it to match the template then stick it in position on the white paper.

04 Stick the light blue bridge to the mid blue bridge with spray adhesive. Stick the bridge to the white paper with spray adhesive, matching the position of the template.

05 Stick the other pieces in place with spray adhesive, matching the position of the template. Remove the template and fix the picture in a picture frame.

VARIATION

A pair of love birds are the ideal motif applied to a sealed envelope containing a Valentine card. The birds are cut from pink paper and applied with spray adhesive.

Sashiko gift tags

Sashiko is a Japanese form of quilting. The stitches were used to strengthen fabric and are highly decorative. The designs are inspired by natural motifs such as flowers and the waves of the sea or are interpretations of family crests. The simple running stitches are also effective when worked on paper. Choose a sturdy paper and pierce through the holes for stitching first. Use the stitched paper to make a smart gift tag for an important present.

YOU WILL NEED

Cutting mat
Thick cream textured paper,
   10 cm (4 in) square
Craft knife
Metal ruler
Tracing paper, 10 cm
   (4 in) square
Black pen
Masking tape
Bradawl
Black stranded cotton
   embroidery thread
Crewel needle
Clear sticky tape
Purple card, 25 x 10 cm
   (10 x 4 in)
Bone folder
5 mm (¹/₄ in) wide double
   sided tape
Cream parchment paper,
   20 x 10 cm (8 x 4 in)
Paper glue

01 Resting on a cutting mat, cut a 6.5 cm (2⁵/₈ in) square of thick cream textured paper with a craft knife and metal ruler. Refer to page 122 to draw a sashiko template on tracing paper with a black pen. Tape the tracing right side up on the square of paper with masking tape. Resting on a cutting mat, pierce a hole at the end of the lines with a bradawl.

02 Thread a crewel needle with four strands of black stranded cotton embroidery thread. Bring the needle to the right side of the square of paper through one of the holes. Stick the thread ends to the wrong side with a piece of clear sticky tape.

03 Refer to the template to sew the sashiko design. To finish, stick the thread ends to the wrong side with a piece of clear sticky tape. Cut off the excess thread. If you need to start a new thread, stick the ends to the wrong side to start and finish.

04 Resting on a cutting mat, cut a 22 x 7.5 cm (8³/₄ x 3 in) rectangle of purple card with a craft knife, cutting against a metal ruler. On the wrong side, score and fold the card 7 cm (2³/₄ in) then 14.5 cm (5¾ in) from the left hand short edge parallel with the short edges using a bone folder.

05 Open the gift tag out flat again. Cut a 5 cm (2 in) square centrally on the centre section, which will be the front. Cut out the square with a craft knife.

VARIATION

This delightful greeting card uses the traditional Sashiko colour scheme of white on indigo and is brightened by framing it on a pink card with a square of origami paper featuring a lively design.

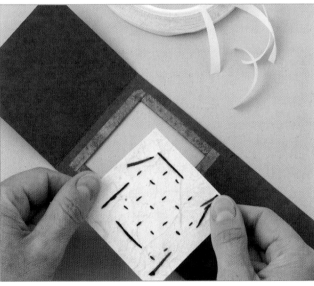

06 Apply double sided tape around the window on the wrong side. Peel off the backing tapes and stick the square under the window. Stick the edges of the left hand section of the card under the front with double sided tape.

07 Resting on a cutting mat, cut a 14 x 6.5 cm (5^1/$_2$ x 2^1/$_2$ in) rectangle of cream parchment paper for an insert with a craft knife, cutting against a metal ruler. Fold the insert in half parallel with the short edges. Run a line of paper glue along the fold and stick inside the gift tag. Stick the tag to the front of the present with double sided tape.

Torn paper paperweight

The delicate art of tearing small pieces of paper to make into pictures has been a popular Japanese papercraft for hundreds of years. Flowers and foliage are favoured motifs. These paperweights feature a leaf sprig of torn papers, delicately coloured with acrylic paint. Glass paperweights with a recess to hold craftwork are available from craft shops.

YOU WILL NEED

Sheet of plastic , 30 x 20 cm
   (12 x 8 in)
Lilac kozo paper, 30 x 20 cm
   (12 x 8 in)
Fine artist's paintbrush
Purple acrylic paint
Cutting mat
Cream Echizen Washi,
   15 cm (6 in) square
Craft knife
Scrap paper
Paper glue
9 cm (3³/₄ in) diameter
   round glass paperweight
Transparent sticky-backed
   plastic, 15 cm (6 in)
   square

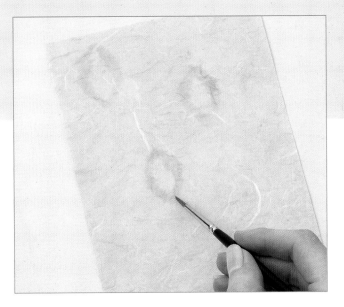

01 Resting on a sheet of plastic to protect your work surface, paint the outline of four leaves on the kozo paper about 4 cm (1³/₄ in) long with a fine artist's paintbrush and water. The water will weaken the paper's fibres.

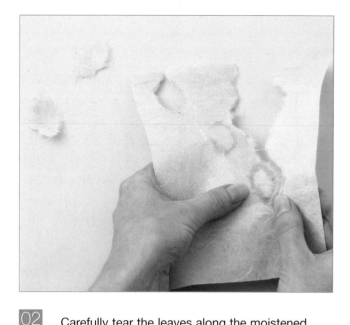

02 Carefully tear the leaves along the moistened outlines.

03 Twist one end of each leaf between your fingers to form a stem.

04 Place the leaves on the plastic sheet and moisten them with water. Use a moistened paintbrush to dab a little purple acrylic paint on the stems. Brush the paint along the stems. It will spread onto the leaves. Leave to dry.

05 Resting on a cutting mat, cut a circle from cream Echizen Washi with a craft knife to fit in the paperweight's recess. Arrange the leaves on the circle. Rest on scrap paper to apply paper glue to the back of the leaves. Stick the leaves to the circle.

VARIATION

Use the torn paper technique to decorate the lid of a small box. Here, orange acrylic paint was applied to yellow paper leaves.

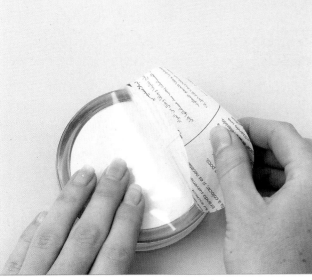

06

Use the paperweight as a template to cut a base from transparent sticky-backed plastic. Place the Echizen Washi circle face down in the recess. Start to peel the backing paper off the sticky-backed plastic circle and position on the back of the paperweight. Press in place then continue peeling off the backing paper to stick it down firmly.

YOU WILL NEED

White tissue paper, 7 sheets,
   25 x 20 cm (10 x 8 in)
Spray adhesive
Stapler
Cutting mat
Bradawl
Light green felt pen
84 white with brown tipped
   stamen strings
2 m 80 cm (112 in) fine
   wire
PVA glue
Cocktail stick
Light green and brown
   flower tape
60 cm (24 in) of
   2 mm ($^1/_{16}$ in) thick wire
Wire snippers

Blossom spray

Branches laden with blossom are a significant symbol of the orient. It is hard to believe that this pretty spray of delicate flowers has petals made from tissue paper. The realistic stamens are called stamen strings which are available inexpensively at craft shops. The flowers are applied to a wire 'branch' and the wire is bound with flower tape which is sold at florist shops.

01 Cut two 22 x 6 cm (8$^1/_2$ x 2$^3/_8$ in) strips of white tissue paper. Stick the strips together with spray adhesive. Use the template on page 122 to trace one flower with a pencil at one end of the strip. Fold the strip in concertina folds with the flower on top. Staple the layers together around the flower. Resting on a cutting mat, use a bradawl to pierce a hole through the centre of the flower.

02 Cut out the flower and separate them into individual flowers. With a light green felt pen, draw a short line along each petal outwards from the centre hole.

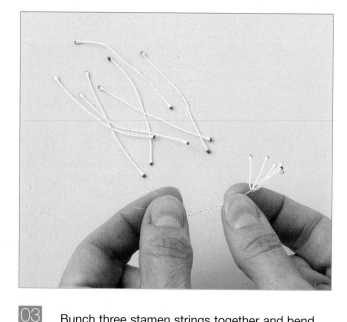

03 Bunch three stamen strings together and bend them in half. Slip a 10 cm (4 in) length of fine wire through the folds. Twist the wires together under the stamen strings.

04 Insert the wire and stamens down through the hole in the flower and adjust the flower to halfway down the stamens.

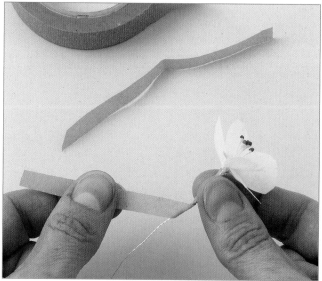

05 Apply pva glue sparingly to the flower around the stamens with a cocktail stick. Gently squeeze the base of the petals around the stamens. Allow the glue to dry then open out the petals.

06 Cut a 10 cm (4 in) length of green flower tape. Cut one end diagonally. Cut the tape lengthwise in half and set one piece aside to use on another flower. Stick the diagonal end to the base of the flower with PVA glue then bind the tape tightly and smoothly around the stamen strings and wire. Cut off the excess tape.

This dainty spray of four blossoms makes a lovely addition to a table setting or gift. The stamens are pink and the white petals have been shaded with a pale pink felt pen at their centre.

07 Make a total of twenty-eight flowers. Bunch the flowers together in seven bunches of four flowers. Snip a 15 cm (6 in) length of 2 mm ($^1/_{16}$ in) thick wire with a pair of wire snippers. Hold one bunch of flowers against the end of the wire and bind in place with brown flower tape. Continue binding the wire, add another two bunches of flowers as you work your way down the wire.

08 Hold a bunch of flowers against the end of the remaining wire which will be the main branch, bind in place with brown flower tape. Continue binding the wire, adding in the other bunches of flowers and the short wire 'branch' as you work your way down the wire.

*1 sheet patterned origami
    paper, 15 cm (6 in) square
2 sheets of different plain
    origami papers, 15 cm
    (6 in) square
Paper glue
White card, 20 x 7.5 cm
    (8 x 3 in)
Bone folder
20 cm (8 in) fine cord
Scissors
Black crepe paper, 10 x 5 cm
    (4 x 2 in)
Pair of tweezers
Flower shaped sequin
Glue dots
Round sequin*

Japanese doll

Paper dolls play a significant role in Japanese Girl's Day celebrations. These charming dolls are so simple to make that you will be able to create a lovely group of dolls using colourful origami papers for their kimonos.

01   Cut a 14 x 9.5 cm (5³/₄ x 3³/₄ in) rectangle from the patterned origami paper and one from one of the plain sheets of origami paper for the kimono. With paper glue, stick the papers together right side up at the centre with one short edge of the plain paper extending above the patterned paper by about 6 mm (¹/₄ in).

02   Use the template on page 123 to cut a doll and a 2.5 cm (1 in) diameter circle for the head from white card. With paper glue, stick the doll centrally on the plain paper kimono with the short overlapped edge level with the neck of the doll. Fold and glue the lower short edge of the kimono up over the lower short edge of the doll.

03 Fold the right hand upper edge then the left hand upper edge of the kimono diagonally over the doll's 'shoulders'. Crease the folds.

04 Fold the right hand edge then the left hand edge of the kimono over the long edges of the doll. Glue the left hand edge in place. Glue the head on top of the neck.

05 Turn the doll over and score across the back 3 cm (1¼ in) above the lower edge with a bone folder. Fold back the lower edge so the doll stands up.

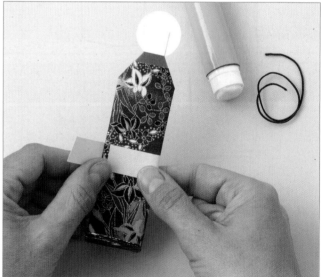

06 Cut a 9 x 1.5 cm (3½ x ⅝ in) strip of the remaining plain origami paper for the obi. Wrap the obi around the doll, overlapping the ends at the back of the doll. Stick the ends in place with paper glue. Tie fine cord around the obi and fasten with a knot at the back of the doll. Cut off the excess cord.

07 Cut a 6.5 x 3 cm (2¹/₂ x 1¹/₄ in) strip of black crepe paper for the hair, cutting the long edges parallel with the paper grain. Fold the hair lengthwise in half then open out flat again. Stick the head centrally on the lower half of the hair and stick in place with paper glue.

08 Refold the hair in half. Fold the ends of the hair diagonally to the front. With a pair of tweezers, stick a flower shaped sequin to the hair with a glue dot. Stick a round sequin on top with a glue dot.

VARIATION

Leave the end of the doll unfolded to make a pretty bookmark.

Japanese bound book

This smart book is constructed using a traditional Japanese binding stitch. Standard writing paper has been used for the pages but you could cut fine handmade paper to size if you prefer. A beautiful oriental printed paper depicting fronds of bamboo has been used for the covers which are decorated with textured papers and a Chinese coin.

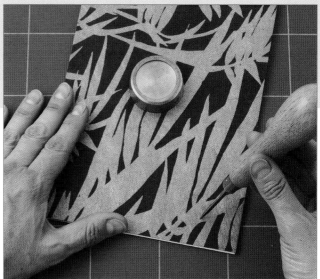

01 Resting on a cutting mat, cut two 25 x 20 cm (10 x 8 in) rectangles of oriental printed paper for the covers using a craft knife and metal ruler. Pile the twelve sheets of white writing paper on the back cover. Place the front cover on top, making sure that all the edges line up.

02 Using a bone folder, score a line on the front cover 2 cm (¾ in) in from the left hand short edge of the papers. This edge will be the spine. Place a weight on the book. Resting on a cutting mat, pierce a row of four equally spaced holes in the scored line through all the layers using a bradawl.

03 Thread a 70 cm (28 in) length of light green linen thread onto a large eyed needle. Slip the needle between the tenth and eleventh pages and insert it through the second hole to bring it out on the front cover. Leave about 10 cm (4 in) of thread between the pages. Insert the needle through the third hole on the front cover. Take it over the book spine and insert it through the third hole again.

04 Insert the needle through the fourth hole on the back cover. Take it over the book spine and insert it through the fourth hole. Take it over the upper edge of the book and insert it through the fourth hole again, bringing the needle out on the front cover.

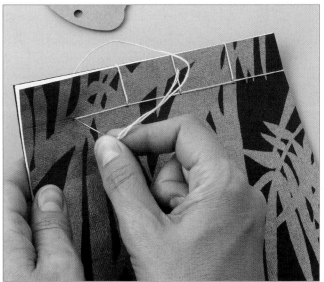

05 Insert the needle through the third hole on the front cover and bring it out of the second hole.

06 Take the thread over the top of the book and insert it through the second hole, bringing the needle out on the front cover. Insert the needle through the first hole on the front cover. Take it over the top of the book and insert it through the first hole, bringing the needle out on the back cover.

The bold red and black colouring is particularly striking on this dramatic book that has covers cut from paper printed with oriental text and red pages. A carved red lacquer bead is sewn to a rectangle of copper coloured paper on a strip of red mulberry paper.

07 Take the thread over the lower edge of the book and insert it through the first hole, bringing the needle out on the back cover. On the back cover, insert the needle through the next hole, bringing the thread out between the tenth and eleventh pages. Open the book and tie the thread ends together in a double knot inside the book. Cut off the excess thread.

08 Tear a 20 x 4.5 cm (8 x 1³/₄ in) strip of white mizutamashi paper. Cut a 3 cm (1¹/₄ in) square of green mulberry paper. Stick the square on the strip 4 cm (1¹/₂ in) above the lower end using spray adhesive. Thread light green linen thread onto a large eyed needle. Sew the coin to the square at two opposite corners. Stick the strip to the front cover. Cut the ends of the strip level with the cover.

Chinese dragon

The fabulous Chinese dragon is a spiritual creature said to control

the weather and symbolises benevolence and good fortune.

This wonderful model can be manipulated with wooden skewers

and its long body is cleverly constructed from circles of tissue

paper. In its mouth is a pearl for good luck.

YOU WILL NEED

*Pale orange card, 40 x
    30 cm (16 x 12 in)*
*Red card, 20 cm (8 in)
    square*
*White card, 10 cm (4 in)
    square*
*Pink paper, 20 cm (8 in)
    square*
Craft knife
Cutting mat
Bold black felt pen
Paper glue
All-purpose household glue
Bone folder
2 wooden skewers
*Pink tissue paper, 70 x
    45 cm (28 x 18 in)*
1 pearl bead

TIP

*See the Cutting Layers of Tissue Paper technique on page
18 for a quick way to cut the tissue paper circles for the body.*

01 Use the template on page 124 to cut one lower head from pale orange card and the flame from pink paper using a craft knife, resting on a cutting mat. Draw the nostrils and cheeks on the lower head and two eyes on white card with a bold black felt pen. Cut out the eyes. Stick the flame around the mouth opening and the eyes to the head with paper glue.

02 Pull the lower edge between a thumb and finger to curve the jaw. Cut two upper heads from red card and two sets of upper teeth and one set of lower teeth from white card. Stick the upper heads under the upper edge of the lower head and the teeth under the mouth opening with all-purpose household glue.

03 Cut the mouth from red card. Score and fold along the broken lines with a bone folder. With the rounded ends of the mouth level with the base of the teeth, stick the tabs inside the head with all-purpose household glue.

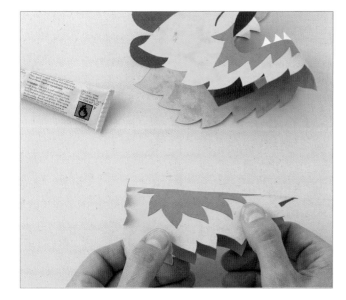

04 Cut one tail from pale orange card and the scales from pink paper. Stick the scales on the tail with paper glue. Pull the short edge between a thumb and finger to curve the tail along the centre. Bend the small points backwards. Stick the remaining points together with all-purpose household glue. Leave the glue to dry.

05 Cut a tail base from red card. Gently squeeze the unglued edge of the tail open. Glue the folded back points to the tail base with all-purpose household glue. Leave the glue to dry.

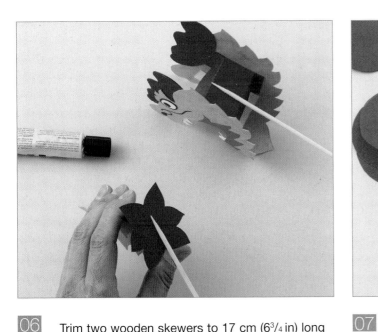

06 Trim two wooden skewers to 17 cm (6³/₄ in) long by cutting off the blunt ends with a craft knife, resting on a cutting mat. Stick the pointed ends of the skewers centrally to the back of the mouth and the tail base with the skewers extending downwards.

07 Cut eighty-five 5 cm (2 in) diameter circles of pink tissue paper for the body. Dab paper glue on the circumference of one circle four times, dividing it into quarters. Press the next circle on top and dab paper glue on the circumference between the positions on the first circle. Continue applying tissue circles one of top of other, alternating the glue positions.

08 Gently pull open the body. Stick the first circle of the body to the back of the mouth and the last circle to the tail base with all-purpose household glue. Stick a pearl in the mouth with all-purpose household glue.

Origami cranes

YOU WILL NEED

15 cm (6 in) square of Lokta paper in five colours

The elegant crane is from an ancient species of birds. It symbolises long life in China and in both Chinese and Japanese mythology the crane is a messenger of the gods to humans. There is a Japanese legend that says that if you fold a thousand paper cranes, the gods will grant your wishes. Master these origami folds and you will see how easy it is create lots of cranes.

01 Fold the square of paper diagonally in half from corner to corner with right sides facing. Unfold the paper then repeat between the other corners. Unfold the paper. Now fold the paper in half parallel with the side edges with wrong sides facing. Unfold the paper and fold it in half again parallel with the other side edges.

02 Unfold the paper but do not flatten it. Bring the four corners of the square to meet, pushing in the side edges.

03 Lift the upper flaps at each side and fold them to meet at the centre. Fold down the top triangle. Unfold the three folds. Turn the paper over and repeat the folds. Unfold the last three folds.

04 Lift the top layer at the lower edge, the upper flaps at each side will fold inwards. Crease along the folds so they lie flat, forming a diamond shape. Turn the paper over and repeat.

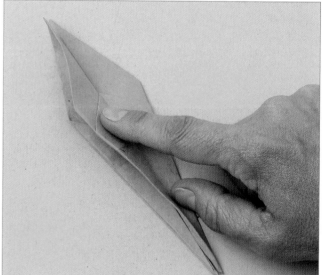

05 Fold the top layers of the paper to meet at the centre. Turn the paper over and repeat.

06 Turn the right hand top layer over the left hand side. Turn the paper over and repeat.

07   Lift the lower point up to meet the top point. Turn the paper over and repeat.

08   Pull the two upper points at each side of the centre outwards and recrease along the base.

09   Fold the upper right hand half over the left hand half. Turn the paper over and repeat.

10   These points will be the head and tail. Fold down the head of the crane. Gently pull open the upper points which are the wings.

Stamped stationery folder

YOU WILL NEED

Cream washi, 40 x 30 cm
  (16 x 12 in)
Oriental rubber stamps
Black and red ink pads
Mounting board, 40 x 25 in
  (16 x 10 in)
Spray adhesive
5 cm (2 in) wide black cloth
  tape
1.5 cm (⅝ in) wide double
  sided tape
1 sheet red cotton paper,
  40 x 25 in (16 x 10 in)
1 red chopstick
Pencil
Cutting mat

Rubber stamping is a very popular craft and there is a wonderful range of images widely available to stamp. The cover of this practical folder is stamped with oriental motifs on lovely Japanese paper and to continue the oriental theme the folder fastens with a chopstick. There are gusseted pockets inside the folder to store paper and envelopes. You could stamp stationery with matching motifs to keep in the folder and send to friends.

01 Cut two 27 x 19 cm (10⅝ x 7½ in) rectangles from cream washi for the covers. Stamp a selection of oriental stamps on one rectangle at least 3 cm (1¼ in) in from the edges for the front cover, stamping one image in black ink and the rest in red ink.

02 Cut two 24 x 17.5 cm (9⅜ x 6⅞ in) rectangles from mounting board. With spray adhesive, stick one board to the wrong side of the front cover 1.5 cm (⅝ in) in from both short and the long left hand edge. Stick the other board to the back cover 1.5 cm (⅝ in) in from both short edges and one long edge. Stick the corners then the edges of the paper to the boards.

03 Cut two 6 cm (2¹/₂ in) lengths of 5 cm (2 in) wide black cloth tape for the loops. Fold each piece of tape lengthwise into thirds with the adhesive sides facing. Stick the ends together with a piece of 1.5 cm (⁵/₈ in) wide double sided tape, forming a loop.

04 Stick each loop to a cover with double sided tape, placing one loop just below the centre and the other loop just above the centre of the long covered edges.

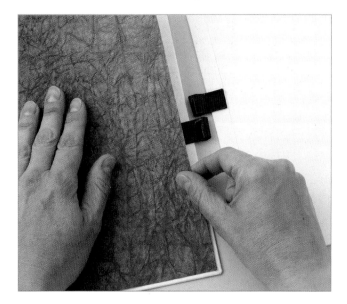

05 Cut two 23.5 x 17 cm (9¹/₈ x 6⁵/₈ in) rectangles from red cotton paper for the linings. Stick the linings centrally to the underside of the covers with spray adhesive.

06 With a pencil, lightly draw a line 1.5 cm (⁵/₈ in) in from the long uncovered edges on both sides of the covers. To make the hinge on the right side, rest on a cutting mat to stick a length of cloth tape to one cover along the drawn line with 1cm (³/₈ in) extending at the top and bottom. Stick the other cover under the other long edge of the tape.

VARIATION

Use a rubber stamp to apply motifs at random to plain paper to create a smart giftwrap.

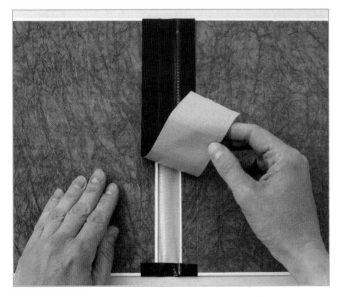

07 Turn the folder wrong side up. Turn the extending ends of tape to the underside and stick down. Stick a 26 cm (10¼ in) length of cloth tape to the hinge, lining up the edges of the tape with the drawn lines.

08 Following the diagram on page 124, cut two pockets from red cotton paper. Stick the hem to the wrong side with double sided tape. Fold the pockets along the solid lines with wrong sides facing and along the broken lines with the right sides facing. Apply double sided tape to the tabs on the right side, peel off the backing tapes and stick the pockets inside the folder.

Fan trimmed giftwrap

The paper fan is a highly stylish motif of the Far East. This pretty fan is very quick to make and is a lovely way of decorating a wrapped present. The struts of the fan are made of Mizuhiki, which is a fine Japanese paper cord.

YOU WILL NEED

2 co-ordinating sheets of Chiyogami, 1 sheet to wrap gift, 20 cm x 10 cm (8 x 4 in) of other sheet for fan
Bone folder
Ruler
5 mm (¹/₄ in) wide double sided tape
Scissors
1 strand of black Mizuhiki
1 strand of gold Mizuhiki
Glue dots

01 Wrap a present with a piece of Chiyogami. Cut a 19 x 6 cm (7⁵/₈ x 2³/₈ in) rectangle of the other Chiyogami for the fan. Score the fan parallel with the short edges 5 mm (¹/₄ in) from each end then at 1 cm (³/₈ in) intervals with a bone folder and ruler. Fold the fan in concertina pleats starting at one end by folding a pleat with right sides facing.

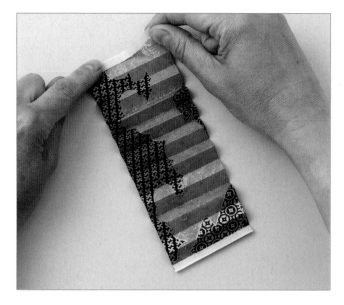

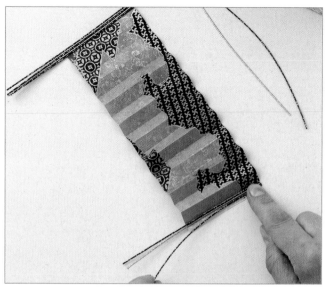

02 Apply 5 mm (¹/₄ in) wide double sided tape to the fan on both sides of the end pleats. Do not remove the backing tapes yet.

03 Cut six 11 cm (4³/₈ in) lengths of black mizuhiki and four 11 cm (4³/₈ in) lengths of gold mizuhiki for the fan struts. Peel the backing tapes off the double sided tape on the right side of the fan. Stick the mizuhiki side by side, alternating the colours on the tape with the upper ends level with the top of the fan.

04 Apply a glue dot 2 cm (³/₄ in) from the extending end of one strut. Stick the other strut on top.

05 Apply another glue dot to the underside of the struts where they intersect. Bind the intersection twice with black mizuhiki. Cut off the ends behind the struts.

VARIATION

A charming contemporary giftwrap has been used to make the fan on this greeting card. A delicate handmade paper embedded with fragments of thread has been applied to white card with spray adhesive to make a folded card which has a strip of light green giftwrap on top to set off the fan.

06

Peel the remaining backing tapes off the fan and stick it to the present.

Paper cut window mobile

Traditionally, paper cut designs are stuck at windows to welcome the new season at the Spring Festival in China. The designs which feature the natural world are passed down through the generations and worked with brilliant inks on fine paper. Recreate a tranquil scene with watercolour paints on watercolour paper then carefully cut it out to hang at a window. The light will show through the delicate cuts.

YOU WILL NEED

Tracing paper, 20 x 15 cm (8 x 6 in)
HB pencil
Watercolour paper, 20 x 15 cm (8 x 6 in)
Masking tape
Selection of watercolour paints
Fine artist's paintbrush
Cutting mat
Craft knife
Sewing thread

TIP

Before cutting out, spray the painting with fixative spray for protection.

01 Trace the template on page 123 onto tracing paper – there is no need to draw the fine details. Turn the tracing over and redraw it on the wrong side with an HB pencil. Tape the tracing right side up on watercolour paper with masking tape. Re-draw the design to transfer it to the paper. Remove the tracing.

02 Paint the flower centres and circles on the butterfly wings with watercolour paints using a fine artist's paintbrush. Leave to dry.

03 Paint the rest of the paper cut, blending the shades together before the paint dries.

04 Resting on a cutting mat, cut out the paper cut with a craft knife. Make sure the blade is sharp as a blunt blade may damage the surface of the paper. Also cut out the small details such as leaf veins and highlights on the petals.

05 Tie a length of sewing thread to the top of the paper for hanging.

VARIATION

The paper cut also works well when cut from plain paper. If you wish to frame the paper cut, apply it with spray adhesive to a contrasting coloured background paper. The rich green hue of this framed paper cut is emphasised by applying it to a pale cream paper.

Padded fish concertina book

Use this charming little concertina book to collect autographs or jot down your thoughts. The stylised koi carp looks as if it is made from padded silk but is actually made from humble mulberry paper. The paper is padded with wadding which is a lightweight material used for quilting. The fish has sequins for scales.

YOU WILL NEED

Cutting mat
Blue pearlised card, 61 x 12 cm (25 x 5 in)
White card, 15 cm (6 in) square
Craft knife
Metal ruler
Bone folder
Wadding, 15 cm (6 in) square
Paper glue
Scissors
Orange, yellow and deep pink mulberry paper, 20 cm (8 in) square
Black relief paint
All-purpose household glue
8 x 4 mm (¹⁄₆ in) pink sequins
Pair of tweezers
Glue dots

TIP

Use bubble wrap, bumpy side down, instead of wadding if you prefer.

01 Resting on a cutting mat, cut a 60 x 10 cm (24 x 4 in) rectangle of blue pearlised card with a craft knife, cutting against a metal ruler. With a bone folder, score the card at 10 cm (4 in) intervals parallel with the short edges. Fold the card in concertina folds along the scored lines.

02 Refer to the template on page 123 to cut the body, head, tail fin, back fin and two front fins from white card. Glue each card piece to wadding with paper glue. Cut the wadding around the card pieces with a pair of scissors.

03 Use the card pieces as templates to cut the pieces from mulberry paper, adding a 6 mm ($^1/_4$ in) margin to all the edges. Hold the padded card pieces centrally on the paper, padded side down, and cut slits around the edges to 2 mm ($^1/_{16}$ in) from the card.

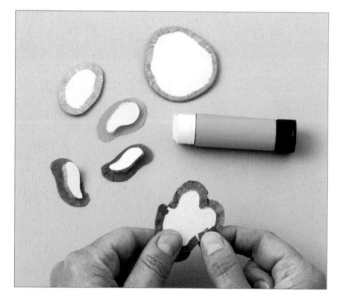

04 Apply paper glue around the edges of the card pieces. Hold the padded card wadding side down on the paper. Fold the paper edges smoothly over the card to cover it. On the small pieces, use the blade of the craft knife to lift and press the paper to the card. Apply more glue as necessary.

05 Draw the eyes on white card. Apply black relief paint to the centre of the eyes as pupils. Set aside to dry then cut out the eyes.

06 Arrange the fish on the front of the book. Stick the body then the other pieces in place with all-purpose household glue.

07 Arrange the sequins on the body of the fish. Use a pair of tweezers to stick each sequin in place with a glue dot.

Weeping willow gift pouch

YOU WILL NEED

Cutting mat
Red pearlised card, 30 x
  20 cm (12 x 8 in)
Craft knife
Metal ruler
Pencil
Gold pen
White relief paint
Bone folder
3 mm (¹/₈ in) hole puncher
1.5 cm (⁵/₈ in) wide
  double sided tape
85 cm (33¹/₂ in) of
  fine gold cord
1.5 cm (⁵/₈ in) diameter
  bead with a large hole

An inro is a container that originally held seals or medicines. They are beautifully decorated and attached with cord to a netsuke, which is a traditional toggle. This charming gift pouch is inspired by an inro embellished with a delicate weeping willow design. A bead slides along the cord to seal the pouch.

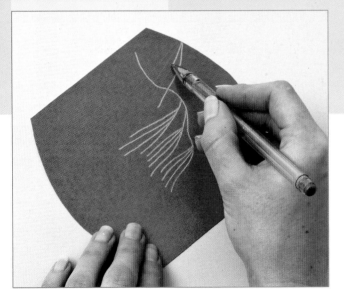

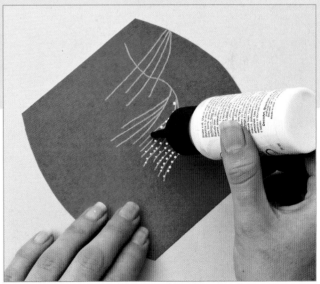

01 Resting on a cutting mat, use the template on page 124 to cut two gift pouches from red pearlised card with a craft knife and metal ruler, cutting one pouch along the broken lines, which will be the back pouch. The pouch with the tabs will be the front pouch. Draw the weeping willow on the front pouch with a pencil. Trace along the drawn lines with a gold pen.

02 Dot white relief paint at random along the weeping willow lines. Set aside to dry. Score along the broken and solid lines with a bone folder.

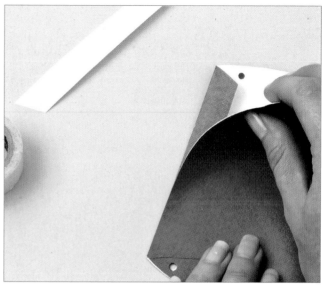

03 Resting on a cutting mat, punch a hole at the dots with a 3 mm ($^1/_8$ in) hole puncher. Fold the pouches with wrong sides facing along the scored lines then open the ellipses out flat again.

04 Apply 1.5 cm ($^5/_8$ in) wide double sided tape to the tabs on the front pouch on the right side. Stick the tabs under the long edges of the back pouch. Gently squeeze the sides of the pouch and fold up the lower back ellipse, then the lower front ellipse.

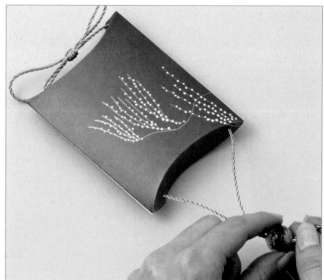

05 Fold the centre of the cord into a figure-of-eight with each loop 5 cm (2 in) long. Tie a knot at the centre.

06 Insert the ends of the cords up through the holes in the lower ellipses, then through the holes in the top back ellipse, and finally the front ellipse. Thread both ends of the cord through a 1.5 cm ($^5/_8$ in) diameter bead with a large hole.

VARIATION

The gift pouch is also very effective without the cord, bead and netsuke as shown on this dainty pouch. The weeping willow is applied with a black felt pen and pink relief paint on pale lilac card.

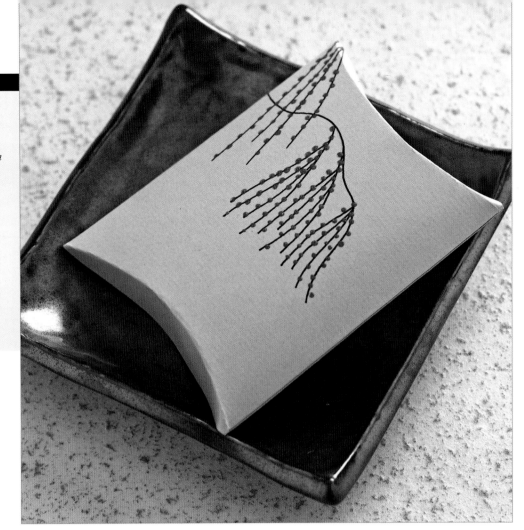

07 Draw two netsuke on red pearlised card. Dot white relief paint at random diagonally across the centre of the netsuke. Set aside to dry.

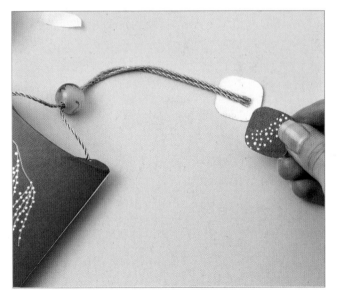

08 Apply double sided tape to the card on the wrong side of one netsuke. Cut out both netsuke. Peel off the backing tapes and stick the ends of the cords to the tape. Stick the netsuke together, enclosing the ends of the cord.

Pagoda box

This model of a handsome Chinese temple has a lift-off lid

so it can be used as a practical container with many uses.

The pagoda is made from coloured card and the lift-off lid

is inventively secured with an oriental bead.

YOU WILL NEED

Cutting mat
Lime green pearlised card,
* 30 cm (12 in) square*
Craft knife
Metal ruler
Bone folder
1.5 cm (⁵/₈ in) wide double
* sided tape*
Dark blue metallic paper,
* 40 x 30 cm (16 x 12 in)*
Spray adhesive
5 mm (¹/₄ in) wide double
* sided tape*
Wooden skewer
Beige paper
Mounting board, 15 x
* 10 cm (6 x 4 in)*
All-purpose household glue
1 cm (³/₈ in) diameter beige
* bead with a large hole*

01 Resting on a cutting mat, use the templates on page 125 to cut the pagoda and pagoda base from lime green pearlised card with a craft knife and metal ruler. Score along the broken lines with a bone folder. Fold along the scored lines with wrong sides facing.

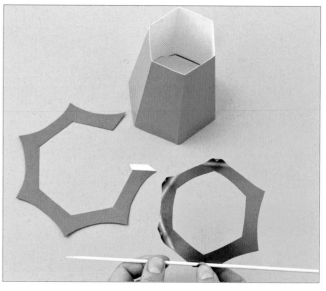

02   Apply 1.5 cm (⁵⁄₈ in) wide double sided tape to the tabs on the right side. Stick the base tabs inside the lower edge of the pagoda. Stick the end tab under the opposite end of the pagoda.

03   Cut out one lower and middle roof from dark blue metallic paper. Stick the tabs under the opposite ends of the roofs with 5 mm (¹⁄₄ in) wide double sided tape. Coil the points of the roofs around a wooden skewer to curl them upwards. Slip the lower then the middle roof over the pagoda. Gently push them as far down the pagoda as they will go.

04   Apply strips of 1.5 cm (⁵⁄₈ in) wide double sided tape to beige paper. Cut out eighteen doors. Peel off the backing paper. Use the tip of the craft knife to stick the doors to each face of the pagoda, centring them at the base and level with the roofs.

05   Apply two pieces of dark blue metallic paper together with spray adhesive and cut out a lid. Apply 5 mm (¹⁄₄ in) wide double sided tape to the tabs. Fold back the face tabs. Peel off the backing tapes and stick the face tabs under the next face of the lid. Stick the end tab under the opposite end. Coil the points around a wooden skewer to curl them upwards.

06 Cut two lid bases from mounting board. Glue the bases together with all-purpose household glue. Cut a lid base from dark blue metallic paper, adding 1.5 cm ($^5/_8$ in) to all edges. Cover the mounting board lid base with the paper using double sided tape.

07 Apply all-purpose household glue to the edges of the lid base. Gently push the base centrally inside the lid. Hold in place whilst the glue dries.

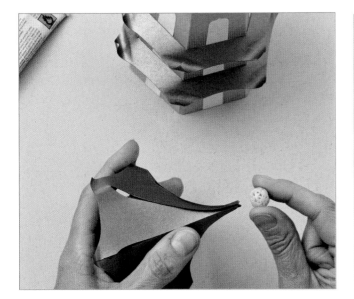

08 Hold the top points of the lid together and dab them with all-purpose glue. Insert the points into a bead with a large hole.

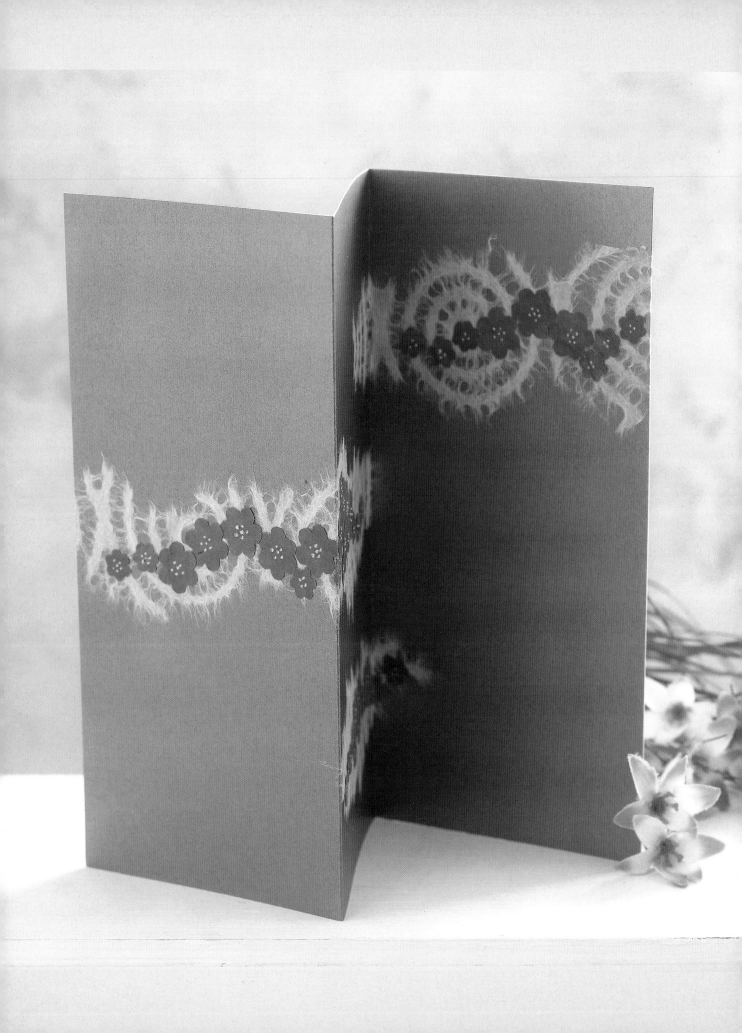

Folding screen greeting card

A Japanese screen with cascades of cherry blossom is the inspiration for this three-fold greeting card. Cherry blossom represents prosperity in Japan so this card would be ideal to send a message of good luck. The blossom is very simple to create as the flowers are stamped with flower shaped paper punches which are available from craft shops.

YOU WILL NEED

*Sheet of gold card, 29.5 x
  21 cm (11¾ x 8⅜ in)
Bone folder
Ruler
White mizutamshi paper,
  30 x 20 cm (12 x 8 in)
Spray adhesive
1.5 cm (⁵/₈ in) flower shaped
  paper punch
1 cm (³/₈ in) flower shaped
  paper punch
Fine pink paper, 20 cm
  (8 in) square
Micro glue dots
Light beige 3D paint*

01 Score the sheet of gold card in thirds parallel with the short edges using a bone folder and ruler. Fold one scored line in the opposite direction to the other to create the screen. Open the card out flat again.

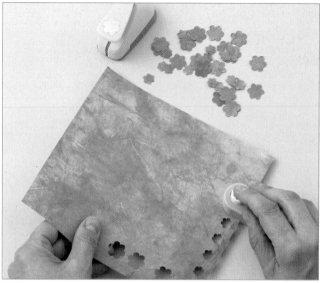

02 Tear white mizutamshi paper at random into three strips. Stick the strips across the screen with spray adhesive. Cut the edges of the mizutamshi paper level with edges of the card if necessary.

03 Use a 1.5 cm ($^5/_8$ in) and a 1 cm ($^3/_8$ in) flower shaped paper punch to punch out about forty flowers from fine pink paper.

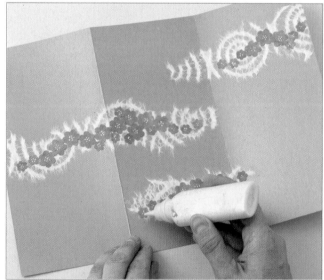

04 Arrange the flowers on the mizutamshi paper strips. Stick the flowers in place with micro glue dots.

05 Apply tiny dots of paint with light beige 3D paint on the centre of the flowers to represent stamens. Leave to dry.

VARIATION

Here is a charming greeting card of autumnal colours made from a folded A5 sheet of cream card. Leaves punched with a leaf shaped paper punch drift across torn bands of handmade paper.

Parasols greeting card

YOU WILL NEED

Dark blue Ogura Japanese paper, 30 x 25 cm (12 x 10 in)

Dark blue card, , 30 x 25 cm (12 x 10 in)

Cream card, 20 x 15 cm (8 x 6 in)

Brown card, 2 cm (¾ in) square

Spray adhesive

Cutting mat

Craft knife

Metal ruler

Bone folder

Turquoise striped Japanese tissue, 25 x 8 cm (10 x 3 in)

Cream patterned paper, 20 x 15 cm (8 x 6 in)

2 different kimono printed papers, 12 cm (5 in) square

Masking tape

Tracing paper

Bradawl

Embroidery needle

Brown stranded cotton embroidery thread

Glue dots

Plain cream paper, 30 x 20 cm (12 x 8 in)

Paper glue

Parasols made of paper and bamboo are a familiar sight in the far East.

Many are beautifully painted and in the past, kings had splendid

parasols that were enormous in size and exquisitely decorated. This

greeting card has a pair of parasols that have a three-dimensional

appearance created by sewing the spokes with embroidery threads.

Books of printed papers are available for craft work. They often use

reproductions of beautiful textiles such as the kimono prints used here.

01 Apply dark blue Ogura Japanese paper to dark blue card with spray adhesive. Resting on a cutting mat, cut a 27 x 20.5 cm (10½ x 8 in) rectangle of the covered card with a craft knife, cutting against a metal ruler. Score the card using a bone folder and fold the card in half parallel with the short edges.

02 Cut a 20.5 x 5.5 cm (8 x 2¼ in) strip of turquoise striped Japanese tissue. Stick to the lower section of the front of the card with spray adhesive.

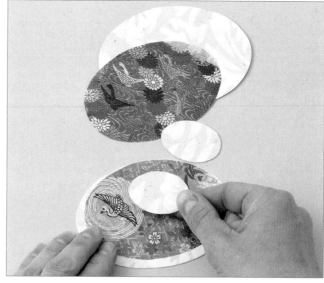

03 Apply cream patterned paper to cream card with spray adhesive. Resting on a cutting mat, use the template on page 124 to cut two parasols A and C of the covered card and two parasols B from two different kimono printed papers with a craft knife. Stick the pieces one on top of the other with spray adhesive to form two parasols.

04 Overlap the parasols and arrange them on the card front. Stick the underlaying parasol in position with spray adhesive. Open the card out flat. Lightly tape a tracing of the template on top with masking tape. Pierce a hole at the dots with a bradawl, the centre holes will need to be large enough to accommodate many strands of embroidery thread. Remove the template.

05 Thread a needle with six strands of brown stranded cotton embroidery thread. Knot the thread end. Starting at the outside edge, sew each spoke between the holes on the outside edge and the centre.

06 Stick the other parasol to the card front. Pierce holes and sew the spokes as before. Cut two small ovals from brown card and stick them over the centre hole with glue dots.

07 Resting on a cutting mat, cut a 25 x 19.5 cm (10 x 7⁵/₈ in) rectangle of plain cream paper for the insert with a craft knife, cutting against a metal ruler. Fold the card in half parallel with the short edges. Stick the insert to the underside of the card front to conceal the stitches using paper glue.

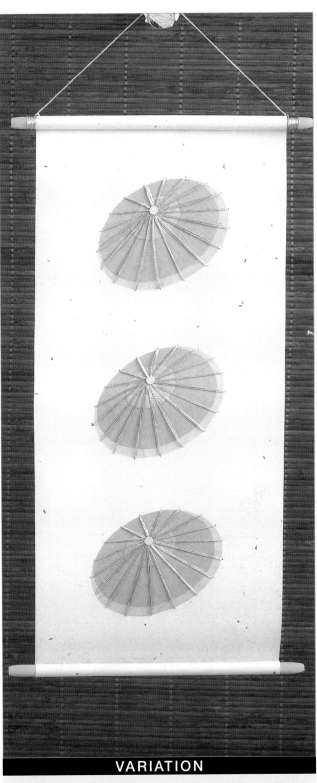

VARIATION

This bright hanging panel of speckled translucent paper has a row of colourful parasols cut from mulberry papers. The ends of the panel are wrapped around lengths of wood dowelling that have been washed with green acrylic paint.

Hexagonal box

This elegant box is very versatile and could be used without the lid as a tub for pens and pencils. The box is held in shape with cleverly tied cords and will fold flat for storage. The lid is topped with a chunky bead tied in place to lift off the lid. The box is covered with a flamboyant Japanese patterned paper and bordered and lined with a co-ordinating plain coloured paper.

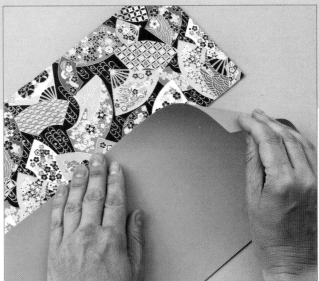

01 Cut a 28.5 x 13.5 cm (11⅝ x 5⅜ in) rectangle of Japanese patterned paper for the box sides. Cut six 12 x 4 cm (4¾ x 1⅝ in) rectangles of mounting board. Stick the boards to the wrong side of the paper 3 mm (⅛ in) apart and 1.5 cm (⅝ in) in from the long lower and short side edges with spray adhesive. Stick the lower and one side edge of the paper over the boards with paper glue.

02 Cut a 27 x 14 cm (11 x 5½ in) rectangle of plain coloured paper for the lining. Spray the wrong side with spray adhesive. With right sides uppermost, lap one long edge of the lining over the upper edge of the box sides for 2.5 cm (1 in). Stick in place.

03 Turn the box sides over and fold the lining smoothly over the upper edge. Stick the lining to the underside of the box sides, pressing it down between the boards.

04 Rest the box sides wrong side up on a cutting mat. With a bradawl, pierce a hole between the first and second board, the third and fourth board and the fifth and sixth board 1.5 cm ($5/8$ in) above the lower edge.

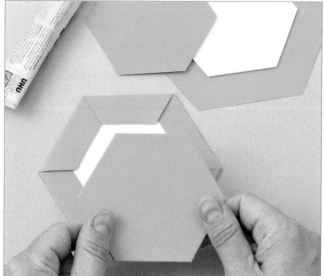

05 Fold the box sides, forming a hexagon. Stick the covered short edge of the box sides over the the extending short paper edge with all-purpose household glue.

06 Referring to the hexagon templates on page 125 cut two bases and one lid from mounting board and one base from plain coloured paper. Stick the board pieces to plain coloured paper. Cut the paper around the board pieces, adding 2 cm ($3/4$ in) to each edge. Stick the paper over the wrong side of the board pieces. Stick one base centrally to the underside of the lid with wrong sides facing.

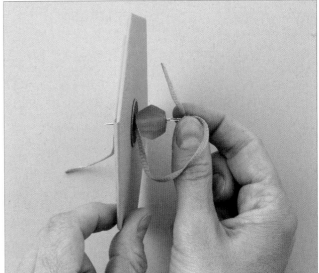

VARIATION

Co-ordinating oriental patterned papers have been used to cover this box and lid which is tied with bright pink cord.

07 Cut three 25 cm (10 in) lengths of cord. Refer to the diagram on page 125 to thread the cords through the pierced holes with a large eyed needle. Adjust the intersection to the centre. Stick the paper base to the remaining base covering the paper edges using spray adhesive. Slip the base into the box and rest it on the cords. Knot the cords close to the box and trim the ends.

08 Rest the lid right side up on a cutting mat. Place the coin on top. With a bradawl, pierce a hole through the centre of the lid and at two opposite corners of the square hole of the coin. Thread the remaining cord up through one side hole, thread on the bead. Thread the cord down through the centre hole and up through the other side hole. Thread the cord through the centre hole. Knot the cord ends.

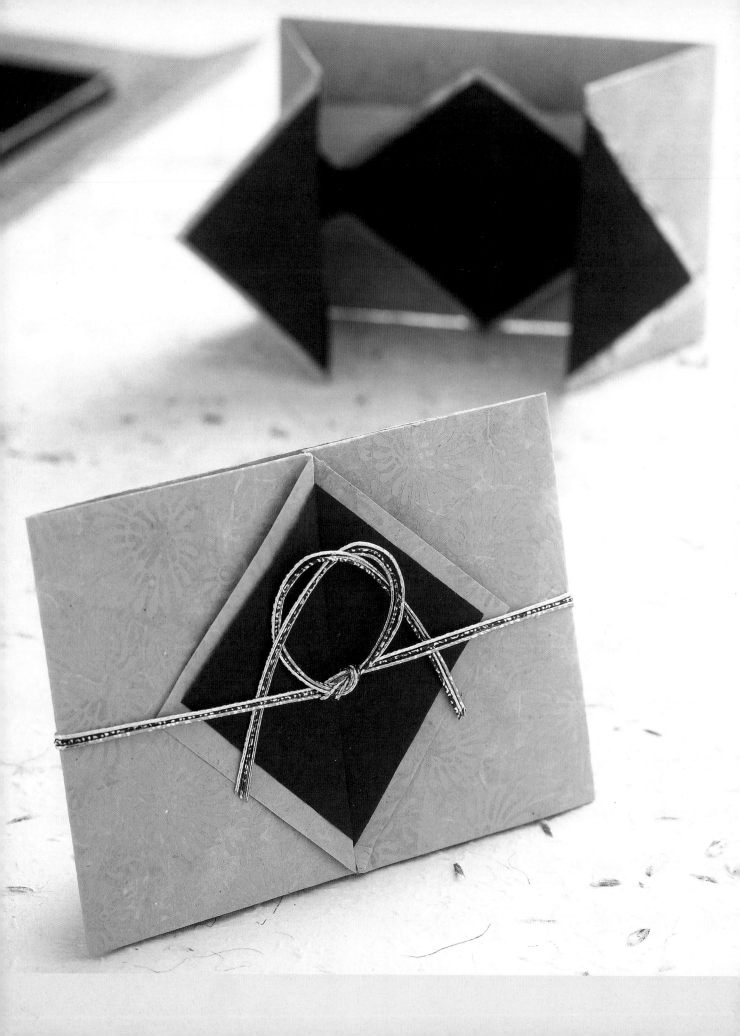

Money wrapper

YOU WILL NEED

Lilac patterned paper, 35 cm
(14 in) square
Purple tissue paper, 35 cm
(14 in) square
Paper glue
Turquoise, purple and silver
Mizuhiki

It is customary in Japan to give gifts of money for all sorts of

occasions. The money is presented in beautifully folded wrappers.

A money wrapper can also be used to present a gift token or as an

envelope for a special greeting card. This money wrapper

is lined with fine tissue paper and fastens with a traditional paper

cord technique.

01 Cut a 30 cm (12 in) square of lilac patterned paper and a 29 cm (1³/₄ in) square of purple tissue paper. Run a line of paper glue along the centre of the tissue paper and stick it centrally to the wrong side of the paper. Fold one corner of the paper diagonally three-quarters of the way along one edge with the tissue paper face to face.

02 Now fold the corner of the paper to meet the centre of the fold with the right sides facing. Open the fold.

03 Fold the paper level with the outer corners parallel with the first fold with right sides facing. Next, refold the paper along the second fold with the tissue paper face to face.

04 Fold the corner to meet the centre of the first fold with the right sides facing. Repeat the folds on the opposite corner of the paper.

05 Turn the paper over and fold back the triangles at each end with right sides facing.

06 Turn the paper over and fold the ends of the wrapper to meet at the centre. Dab paper glue sparingly on the tissue paper corners to hold them in place. Open the wrapper and slip the money or other gift inside. Refold the wrapper.

VARIATION

Here is a pastel coloured money wrapper lined with gold tissue paper. If you do not have Mizuhiki paper cord, use memory cord instead as shown here.

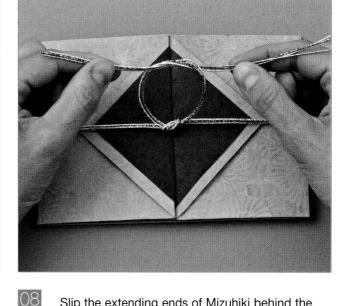

07 Cut a 65 cm (25½ in) length of turquoise, purple and silver Mizuhiki. Place the Mizuhiki under the wrapper and fold the ends over the front and fasten them with a double knot. Lift the ends and overlap them in a single knot above the double knot.

08 Slip the extending ends of Mizuhiki behind the tied cords. Cut off the ends diagonally.

Chrysanthemum trims

These delightful, stylised chrysanthemums can be used to decorate all sorts of items. The chrysanthemum represents purity and longevity throughout Asia and is an especially important symbol in China and Japan. It has been the national flower of Japan for many centuries. Here, the chrysanthemums are applied to a giftwrapped present on a band of Japanese paper.

01 Wrap a boxed present with copper fibres washi. Wrap a 5.5 cm (2¼ in) wide strip of white floral printed washi around the present. Overlap the ends of the paper under the present and stick together with double sided tape.

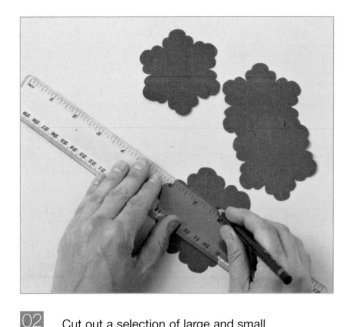

02 Cut out a selection of large and small chrysanthemums from red with orange fibres washi using the templates on page 125. Mark the solid and broken lines lightly on the wrong side with a pencil and ruler.

03 Fold the chrysanthemums with wrong sides facing along the solid lines then along the broken lines, open out flat after each fold.

04 Push the triangles in toward the centre of the chrysanthemum then fold all the petals in the same direction to flatten the chrysanthemum.

05 Arrange the chrysanthemums on the present then stick them in place with double sided tape.

VARIATION

In Japanese flower language, white chrysanthemums symbolise faith. This greeting card of Japanese papers features a row of white folded chrysanthemums.

Chopsticks wrapper

Paper chopstick wrappers are a lovely addition to a table setting for a celebratory oriental meal. Choose a lightweight paper that will fold smoothly such as this beautiful Tibetan printed paper. Insert the pointed ends of a pair of chopsticks into the wrapper.

 Cut a 30 x 20 cm (12 x 8 in) rectangle of Tibetan printed paper. Fold the paper in half parallel with the long edges with wrong sides facing. Open out flat again. Fold the left hand long edge to meet the centre fold.

02 Turn the paper over. Fold the top and bottom right hand corners diagonally to meet the centre fold with right sides facing. Open out flat again. Fold the corner to meet the centre of the diagonal fold with right sides facing.

03 Refold the first diagonal folds. Fold the paper diagonally matching the second diagonal fold to the first diagonal fold.

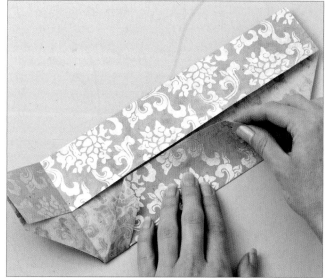

04 Turn the paper over. Fold up the lower edge for 5 cm (2 in). Open the fold out flat again.

05 Fold the right hand long edge to meet the centre fold with wrong sides facing then open the fold.

 06   Fold up the lower edge. Wrap the right hand edge over the back of the wrapper.

07   Turn the paper over and fold the lower square to the front of the wrapper. Cut a 4.5 x 2.5 cm (1³/₄ x 1 in) rectangle of cream card. Apply a glue dot to the wrong side at the upper edge. Slip the card behind the pleats at the lower right hand edge of the wrapper. Press the upper edge to the wrapper. Stick an oriental token on top with a glue dot.

VARIATION

Using a brightly patterned paper that is white on the wrong side emphasises the pleats, as shown on this wrapper made from Japanese patterned paper.

Templates

All templates are shown at 50%

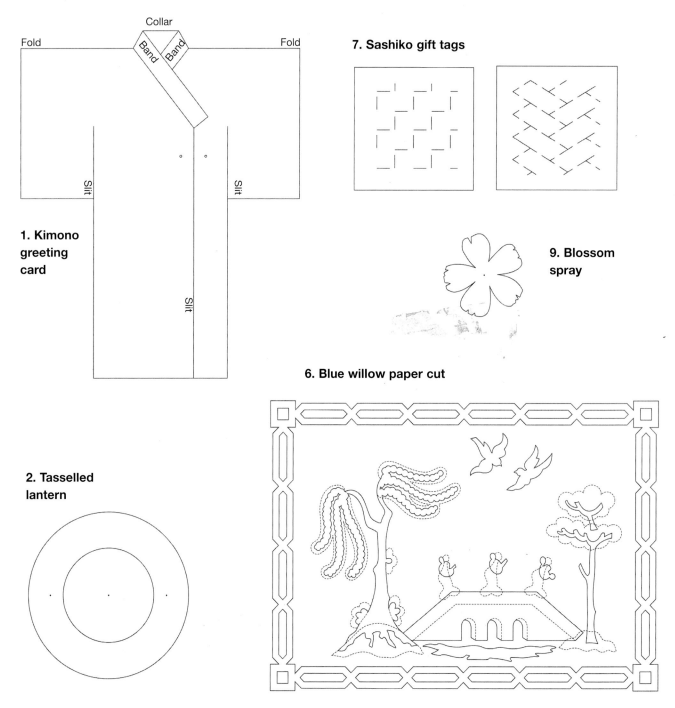

Collar

Fold

Band Band

Fold

Slit

Slit

Slit

1. Kimono greeting card

2. Tasselled lantern

7. Sashiko gift tags

9. Blossom spray

6. Blue willow paper cut

10. Japanese doll

16. Padded fish concertina book

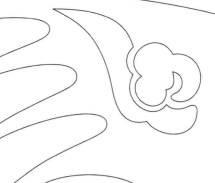

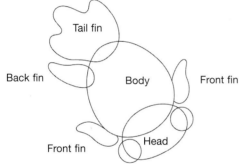

Tail fin

Back fin

Body

Front fin

Front fin

Head

4. Stencilled butterfly kite

Wing

Body

15. Paper cut window mobile

5. Origami box

Lid

Box

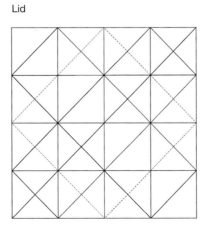

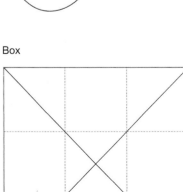

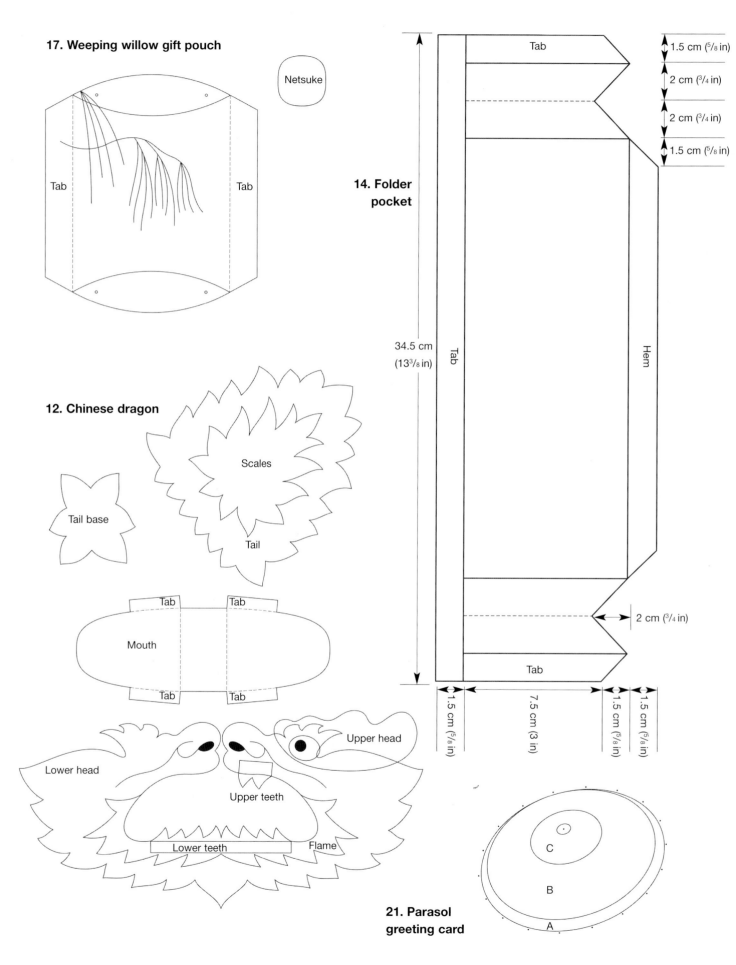

17. Weeping willow gift pouch

Netsuke

Tab   Tab

14. Folder pocket

Tab

1.5 cm (⁵/₈ in)

2 cm (³/₄ in)

2 cm (³/₄ in)

1.5 cm (⁵/₈ in)

Tab

Hem

34.5 cm (13³/₈ in)

2 cm (³/₄ in)

Tab

1.5 cm (⁵/₈ in)

7.5 cm (3 in)

1.5 cm (⁵/₈ in)

1.5 cm (⁵/₈ in)

12. Chinese dragon

Scales

Tail base

Tail

Tab   Tab

Mouth

Tab   Tab

Upper head

Lower head

Upper teeth

Lower teeth

Flame

21. Parasol greeting card

C

B

A

124

Middle roof

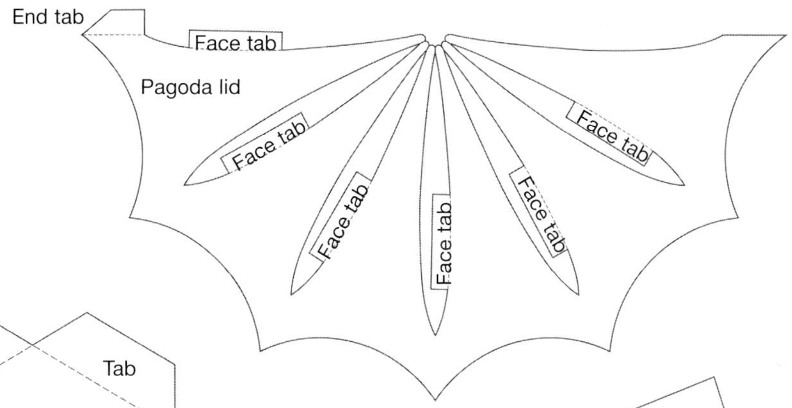

End tab

Face tab

Pagoda lid

Face tab

Face tab

Face tab

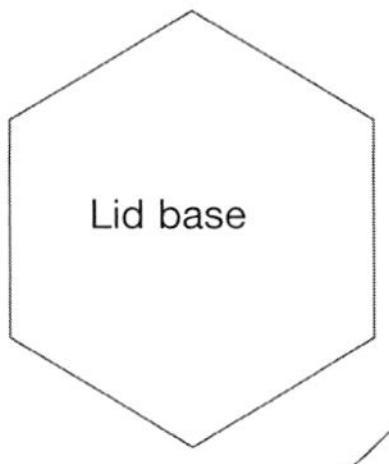

Face tab

Face tab

Tab

Tab

Tab

Tab

Tab

Lid base

Pagoda base

Tab

Tab

18. Pagoda

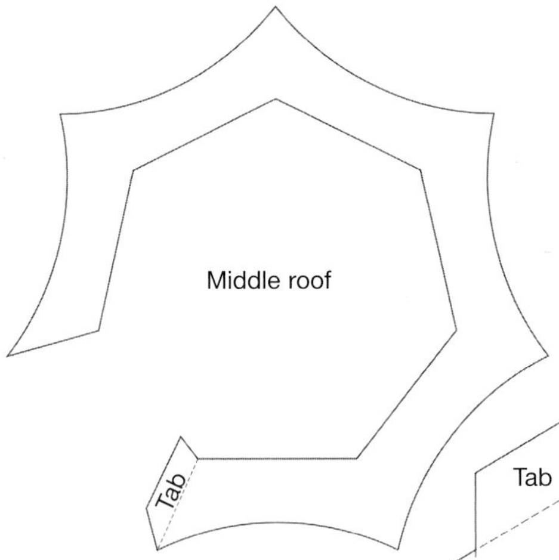

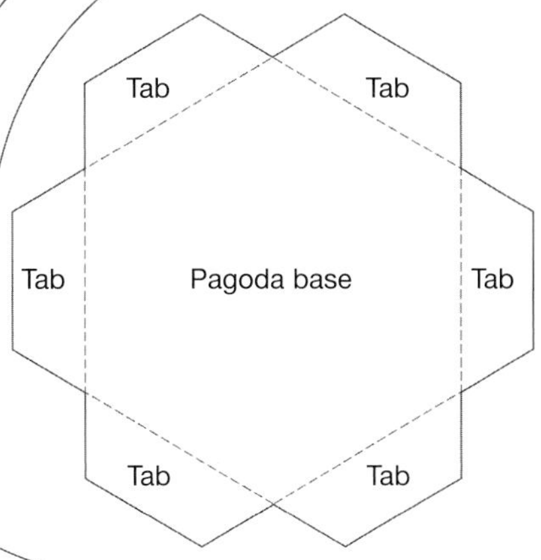

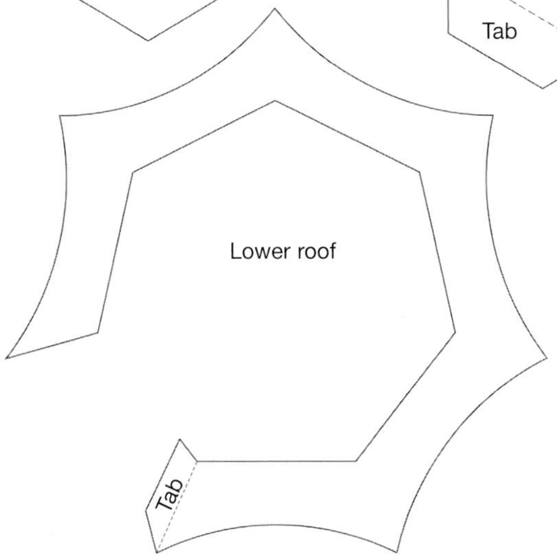

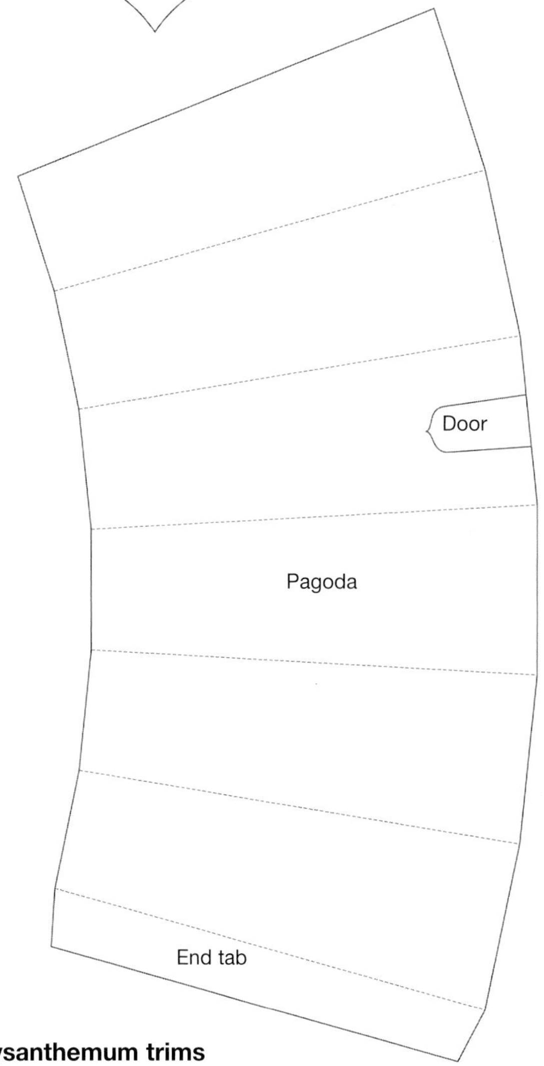

Door

Pagoda

Lower roof

Tab

End tab

22. Hexagonal box

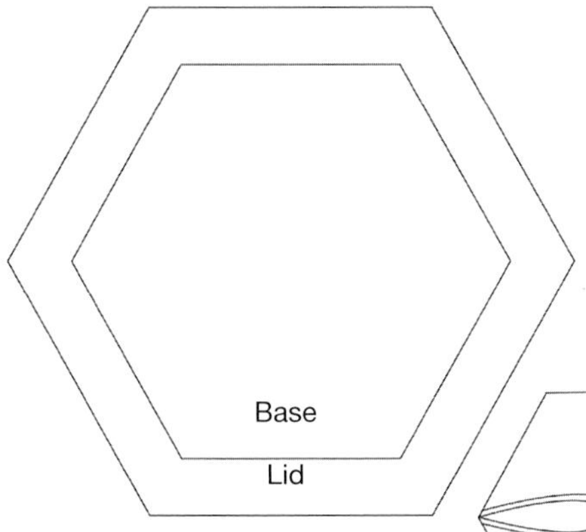

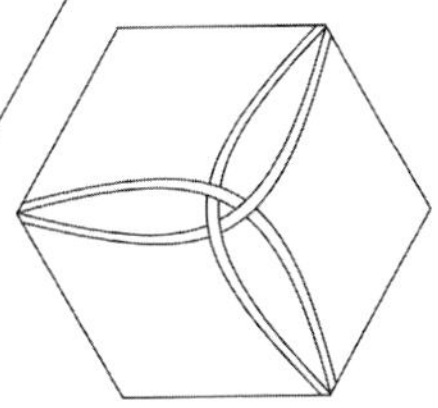

24. Chrysanthemum trims

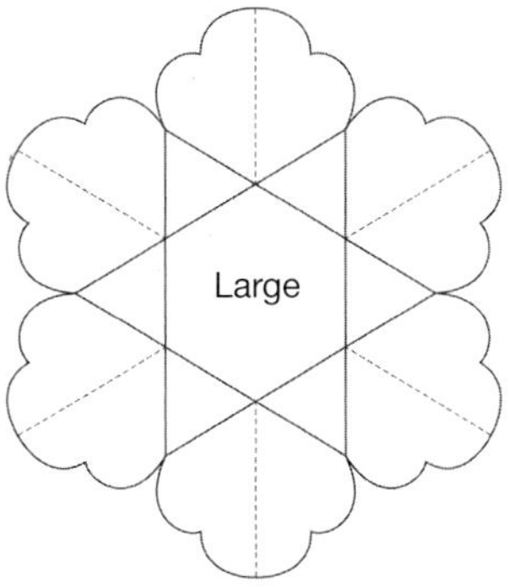

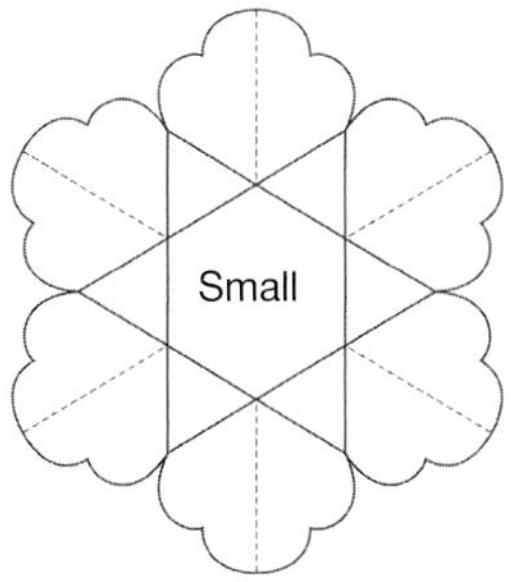

Base

Lid

Cord diagram

Large

Small

Suppliers

UK

Falkiner Fine Papers
Tel: 0207 831 1151
for specialist papers and book
binding materials

Fred Aldous
www.fredaldous.co.uk
Tel: 0161 236 4224
for craft materials

The Japanese Shop
www.thejapaneseshop.co.uk
Tel: 01423 879888
for Japanese patterned papers
and Hizuhiki

Paperchase
Tel: 0207 467 6200
for specialist papers

The Scientific Wire Co.
www.wires.co.uk
Tel: 0208 505 0002
for coloured wires

USA and Canada

Art Supply Warehouse
Art and craft supplies
www.aswexpress.com

Fiskars Brands, Inc.
General craft materials and tools
www.fiskars.com

Stampendous, Inc.
Rubber stamps
www.stampendous.com

South Africa

Arts, Crafts and Hobbies
General supplier
72 Hibernia Street, George 6529
Tel: 044 874 1337

Crafty Supplies
Shop UG 2, Stadium on Main,
Main Road, Claremont 7700,
Cape Town
Tel: 021 671 0286

Australia and New Zealand

LIncraft
General craft supplier.
Stores throughout Australia
www.lincraft.com.au

Fine Art Papers
Artist materials and special papers
200 Madras Street, Christchurch, NZ
Tel: 03 379 4410

Index